WE ARE
GENERATION
Z

WE ARE GENERATION

Z

How Identity, Attitudes, and
Perspectives Are Shaping Our Future

VIVEK PANDIT

BROWN BOOKS
PUBLISHING GROUP

We Are Generation Z: How Identity, Attitudes, and Perspectives Are Shaping Our Future

Brown Books Publishing Group
16250 Knoll Trail Drive, Suite 205
Dallas, Texas 75248
www.BrownBooks.com
(972) 381-0009

A New Era in Publishing™

ISBN 978-1-61254-218-8
Library of Congress Control Number 2015945494

Printed in the United States
10 9 8 7 6 5 4 3 2 1

For more information or to contact the author, please go to
www.WeAreGenZ.com

To my fellow Gen Zers—once we understand who we are, together we will accomplish great things.

Contents

Acknowledgments

Writing my first book was a journey that I began in my freshman year of high school at the age of fourteen, and one I completed two years later as a junior. As other authors have experienced, the process of writing a book is one of self-discovery. In my case, the process was also about discovering a new generation that is emerging: Generation Z. This path of self-discovery, both on an individual and also on a generational level, could not have been possible without the help and expertise of the following people:

My family. My dad was the spark that ignited my passion for writing and the one who suggested I consider transforming my journal entries into a book. My mom's encouragement for me to set my own deadlines—and then her knack for showing me how to adhere to them—was the key to remaining on course throughout the whole publication process. My sister expanded my perspectives on many of the issues I have written about. She has been wholeheartedly cheerful and supportive in a way that only a sister could be.

My grandparents. My grandparents are part of the remarkable "Silent Generation." Their journey through life is full of such incredible stories that I can now see the world through their eyes, with a view that is quite distinct from other generations. My paternal grandfather in particular, as an author and a speaker, offered practical advice that was invaluable.

My cousins. My Gen Z cohorts, who are all younger than me: thank you for letting me peer into your lives and appreciate who we are and who we will become.

My friends. Our candid conversations helped shape my understanding of our generation, and without this constant dialogue, I would not have had the material for a book.

Bryan Mark Rigg. Dr. Rigg, an author, historian, retired US Marine officer, and graduate of Yale and Cambridge Universities, has been my mentor throughout my high school years. His dedication to helping me discover my passions has been unwavering. I thank him for agreeing to read my manuscript and for writing the foreword.

The Brown Books Publishing Group. I am very appreciative of their work in transforming my manuscript into a published book. Knowing that a successful and reputable company had faith in me was an amazing feeling. My editor, Lucia Retta, challenged me to think critically and to look at issues from as many perspectives as possible. Thank you for your frank feedback throughout the process.

Foreword

I have known Vivek Pandit for his whole life. He comes from a family with deep roots in Kashmir, Afghanistan, and southern India. His family embraces a proud culture following the tenets of religious pluralism, tolerance, and kindness. The way they interact with their community is a true testament that they believe in the American dream that "all men are created equal." In fact, the story of his family in America shows the power of the democratic ideals of diversity, industry, and education. I went to school with his uncle, Rahul Pandit, and his aunt, Lavannya Pandit, at Yale University. In fact, Lavannya is my wife's good friend and former roommate from Yale, so we have known of the family and been friends with certain members of it for over two decades.

Knowing Vivek's background, it is not surprising how accomplished he is at the young age of seventeen. He comes from a tradition of hard work and intelligence in action, and he has taken on a huge task in trying to explain his generation, Generation Z, to the broader public with this book.

This generation is dominated by technology, and unlike other generations, it is communicating with each other about ideas at incredible speeds. Whereas a hundred years ago, it took weeks to report on events in the world, today, we learn about events halfway across the globe within seconds. In fact, Generation Z is learning more and more about less and less all the time. It, unlike other generations, learns of current events and scientific breakthroughs in real time and absorbs more than most generations simply by the fact that the information is accessible on their computers. A hundred years ago, one had to travel to elite universities to study difficult topics with accomplished professors. Today, with a click of the mouse, one can enter the world of prestigious universities and learn what the students are learning there. If a person wants to learn something difficult, he or she can download the information almost instantly using the vast library accessible through any Internet connection.

In this age of such broad exposure to the world through technology, a remarkable transformation is also occurring which Vivek discusses persuasively: the evolution of tolerance for diverse lifestyles and beliefs within Generation Z simply through exposure. Of course, Vivek realizes that there is much work to be done in the world—one just has to look at the ISIS movement in the Middle East and its religious racism, intolerance, and genocide—but he also describes how far the United States has come since Martin Luther King, Jr. and how social media helps to stamp out racism quickly in the age of texting, tweeting, and video chatting.

Vivek shows that his generation, through the use of the Internet, will revolutionize how people think and view others simply by the fact that more and more people are being exposed to diverse backgrounds, unique educational experiences, and other religions. The fact that many teenagers in Texas worry about racial, gender, and sexual inequality and want everyone to be aware of these issues and fight against discrimination is a sign that Generation Z is probably more open-minded and socially aware than any previous generation to have existed. One can argue that if there is a generation to help move mankind forward to truly believe that there is one race, the human race, Generation Z has the best chance of doing so. And Vivek does a nice job of showing how it might accomplish this lofty goal.

Bryan Mark Rigg, PhD
Author of *Hitler's Jewish Soldiers:*
The Untold Story of Nazi Racial Laws
and Men of Jewish Descent in the German Military

Sometimes it falls upon a generation to be great. You can be that great generation.

—*Nelson Mandela*

Introduction

I was born at the turn of the millennium. I listen to music mainly by streaming it but occasionally purchase songs online. I have watched movies on DVD but prefer instant downloads. I grew up thinking the war on terror always existed but mostly in the background of life. My phones have always had touch screens.

To connect with family and relatives, I will occasionally use Facebook, but to communicate with friends, I rely on Instagram, Snapchat, and Twitter. For a conversation with one person or a small group, I prefer texting on my phone, although to contact my teachers or relatives I will use e-mail. For a while, I thought e-mail was what people meant when they referred to "snail mail." Eventually I realized that snail mail was the paper stuff that goes through the post office, taking days to reach someone. I call that "ancient mail."

When I need to do research for a homework project, I go to the Internet. I can now distinguish between websites with poor information and websites that are excellent resources. If I need to collaborate with others on this project, I know video hangouts work well.

The problem with so many modes of communication is that sometimes I do not always choose the best option. I might skirt a potentially serious discussion by using an emoticon. I may also be fixated with the continuous present, with whatever is happening *now*, believing that I can multitask and navigate multiple topics better than anyone from a previous generation. Given the option of constant communication, I like having constant feedback—and I also like to offer feedback, such as through online reviews. I also love to shop online, taking time to explore multiple sites and examine multiple reviews before deciding on the best option.

So who am I? In a nutshell, I am Generation Z, those born after the Millennial generation. Generations are loosely defined, not just in terms of biology but also in terms of history and technology. Based on these factors, a generation spans roughly two decades. Most experts agree that the birth of Generation Y members, or the Millennials, spanned the 1980s and most of the '90s. But a distinct set of historical and technological factors near the start of the new millennium has spawned a new generation, Gen Z. And that is where I enter.

So what is the difference between Gen Y and Gen Z? Mark Zuckerberg, for example, is a member of Gen Y. Gen Z members, on the other hand, identify with Adora Svitak, a brilliant young author and advocate for literacy and youth empowerment. Her TED talk, "What Adults Can Learn from Kids," has received over three million views and has been translated into forty languages.

Svitak's popularity is partly based on a notion that Gen Z is already aware of, the notion that technology has leveled the playing field across generations and around the world. Thanks to the role of technology in our lives today, creative, innovative thoughts sparked by teenagers no longer have to be filtered and processed through another generation's prism in order to garner public feedback or serve the public interest.

The impact of this technology in our daily lives cannot be overstated. Our lives are being influenced by technology in ways that haven't occurred in decades. For instance, since the invention of cars, we have relied on gasoline—yet I see the possibility of never having to drive a gasoline-powered car as an adult. And I may even have choices in this regard, ranging from currently available electric cars to the future availability of hydrogen-powered or solar-powered vehicles.

Moreover, with other technologies on the rise, such as 3-D printing and drones, the sky is the limit in what we can achieve. My generation will be able to bring ideas, services, and products to the public faster than any other generation, and we will be able to fund our ideas more quickly with online support such as crowdfunding in order to make them a reality.

But we also have some concerns. We are concerned about the uncertain structure of the world we live in. During our years, we have seen rapid and significant changes in governments and nations around the world. The Berlin Wall may have taken over twenty-five years to crumble, yet my generation has seen a similar worldwide impact after just one Arab Spring. We realize that such rapid changes can affect everything from the price of gas to national security. We understand that with national security concerns come increasing government surveillance, which is a fact we accept but of which we are also wary.

Most importantly, we are cautious of our permanent digital footprints. We see the digital world as an extension of our real worlds, a place to create an extended identity, a place where we want to experiment, be creative, and express ourselves fully and unconditionally. But we do not want those words to come back and haunt us years or even moments after in the wrong context.

We are also concerned about the economy, having grown up most of our lives witnessing the struggles of Millennials such as our older siblings who experienced difficulty finding jobs or had to return home to live. We thus realize that, unlike our parents or grandparents, we may not be with the same company for years on end and we certainly don't expect a pension. We also do not want to spend decades paying off student loans. Our concerns are reflected in the books and movies we like. It is no wonder that apocalyptic story lines featuring young adults, such as the Hunger Games series or the Divergent series, are popular with us.

But we are not pessimistic, and we are not isolationist. Contrary to popular belief, we are not always staring at our phones, and we actually enjoy the company of people.

We just interact differently. Most of us have a pretty good relationship with our parents. Especially given the economy, we are accustomed to living with grandma, grandpa, older siblings, and our parents all in the same household.

We are also very tolerant. We may not agree with everyone's views, but we accept them. Our attitudes have changed, and we are now more concerned about the motives of governments, corporations, and other groups in power than we are of an individual with opposing beliefs. Issues of gender and race are less important to us simply because our perspective is that they should not be issues at all.

Since we are closely connected with people and cultures from around the world, we appreciate the elements that are common to all humans. Barriers such as language are just another firewall that can eventually be taken down to reveal a humanity that is craving the same things—peace, love, happiness, and security.

With Generation Z now poised to reach adulthood, our impact in the global arena will soon be felt. But what makes us tick? What are the issues that matter to us? The answers to these questions lie in understanding how our identity is forming, how our attitudes are taking shape, and how our perspectives are developing. As I explore these topics, many of the issues I discuss are enduring issues of humanity that each generation before me has addressed. However, my peers and I are growing up in a hyperconnected world where the rapid proliferation of technology and global access to information are influencing our attitudes and perspectives like no generation before us. Thus, the aim of my book is to explore the identity, attitudes, and perspectives of Gen Z—from the point of view of someone who is growing up in the midst of this generation.

Life isn't about finding
yourself. Life is about
creating yourself.

—*Unknown*

Part 1

Identity

First I was born. Next I was given a name, first, middle, and last: Vivek Srinivasan Pandit. My race and ethnicity were already bestowed upon me. My gender was not something I chose, but something I received. At birth, my eyes were brown and my hair was black; I had ten fingers and ten toes, two legs, and two arms. All these characteristics were decided without my personal influence. My genetic makeup as a whole was created without my say. Beyond that, my family background and cultural influences had already begun to shape all that I was without my conscious understanding. My parents' home, soon to be mine, was already established. My home country and the part of the world I lived in were already planned. When I first opened my eyes, I saw the parents that created me. I had to be theirs; I had *no choice*. All of this, my predetermined identity, was something I couldn't control, something unalterable. But as I grew older, from infant to teen, I noticed that my identity also grew or, better stated, evolved. My identity was thus no longer resolute. I began to see that I could control who I was and who I could become.

By the time I was an adolescent, I identified myself as a well-rounded, smart, vegetarian, Indian-American kid. I considered myself funny since my mom laughed at all my jokes. I believed I was athletic because I could "beat" my dad in a race. I joined a soccer team and later a football team, and sports became a part of who I was. All my cousins in India called me "the football man" (owing to the fact that the American version of football doesn't exist in India). I began to excel in academics in the third grade, and being "above average" became part of my identity as well. As a child, it seemed that whatever activity in which I participated helped shape me into who I became.

By the time I entered middle school, the factors affecting my identity were more complicated. I no longer thought I was funny simply because my mom would laugh at my jokes. I no longer considered myself fast because I could beat my dad in a race.

Instead, my identity revolved around what a wider group of others thought of me. Even my personal opinion of my own rank and grades didn't seem as significant as my classmates' opinions. And although I did not view myself as highly intelligent or gifted, some classmates perceived me in that manner, and I suspect it affected their behavior toward me. This, in turn, affected my perception of my own capabilities.

Looking back, even my personality was affected by others' perceptions and preconceptions. With my family I was outgoing and silly and did not care about doing "funny-stupid" things. But with my friends, I was more reserved. When there was an opportunity for me to try out for a school play, my parents were shocked that I was not interested because they saw me as full of expression and quite theatrical.

When I reached high school, my peers and I found it was imperative for us to connect with each other through social media. How else were we supposed to know "she dumped him" or "they are going out for the third time"? Facts about us traveled swiftly in cyberspace, giving rise to opinions about each other that developed within minutes instead of over days or weeks. And when these opinions were posted on various social media platforms, they characterized our personalities more harshly than what we would expect after a face-to-face interaction. More alarming was the fact that the perceptions posted on social media would now heavily bias any subsequent face-to-face communication we had with each other.

So as my peers and I relied more and more on the Internet to communicate our opinions of each other, my high school years strengthened the impact of my peers on the identity I chose to display to them. For example, if a friend takes a strong stance on an issue and posts his view online, I might be less inclined to post an opposing view. I might be even less inclined to broach the topic face-to-face with him since I was already aware of his opinion. Prior to the online era, we would have likely discussed the issue in a more interactive, back-and-forth process that might lead to a better appreciation of each other's perspectives, even if at the end of the conversation our views remained different. However, in the online era, the written word is often viewed as conclusive and inalterable. Opinions posted online are not so much up for discussion as they are for argument, and once a view is expressed, it is usually held to be true.

Furthermore, if a friend said he thought I was humorous or my peers shared this view online, then I became more likely to post additional humorous thoughts as well. I would also tend to adjust my behavior in a similar manner in direct, personal situations as well. And while face-to-face communication still existed, my digital self seemed to play an ever-increasing role in how I was perceived and thus in how I perceived myself. Our digital identities, in fact, are becoming progressively more combined with the definition of who we are. The traditional factors that used to shape our identities—real-world experiences, real-world friendships, relationships with parents and extended family—are now being supplanted by factors borne out of the online experience. How many likes, shares, and views I had defined my popularity more than the number of kids I hung around with did.

So in this first part of the book, I will delve into the impact that the technology revolution has had on who we are as people—our thoughts, feelings, and actions—both as individuals and as a society. In chapter 1, I will discuss the rampant use of technology in our everyday lives from my perspective as a teenager. I will also address the negative side effects of technology, including how it may stunt language growth, interfere with education, and potentially lead to an identity crisis. In chapter 2, I will discuss the safety concerns that accompany our use of technology, the positive and negative sides of portraying oneself via technology, and the shift from a social to an online personality. In chapter 3, I will explore how being entrenched in the online era is also affecting our offline identities.

Chapter 1

Technology Domination

One summer, I flew to Chicago to visit my grandparents and cousins. I was particularly excited since I would be seeing my then two-year-old baby cousin for the first time in more than six months. On the plane, I envisioned her first glimpse of me, which always turned into a joyous scream and a big, beaming smile. When I walked into my grandparents' home, I dashed over to her side. She was holding an iPhone, which I instinctively pried from her hands as I knelt down to give her a big hug. Imagine my surprise as she resisted—and then threw a fit because I had taken away her gadget.

Flustered and dejected, I returned her iPhone and moved on to greet the rest of the family.

For the remainder of my two-week summer trip, I noticed how frequently my two-year-old cousin entertained herself with either an iPad or a smartphone. She was so obsessed with her digital entertainment devices that her verbal communication mostly consisted of "Can I have your *pone*?"

The thought of my little cousin developing a closer relationship with her iPad than with me during our summer bonding trip was somewhat unsettling. *Is this the norm, or is she an anomaly?* I wondered. So I researched the issue and found two excellent articles that confirmed my suspicions. These sources indicated that others have also observed similar changes in behavior and communication that technology creates in children. The learning of specific communication techniques is in fact being hampered by technology, delaying a toddler's ability to talk.

The first article I reviewed was from the *New York Times*, called "The Child, the Tablet, and the Developing Mind."[1] Drawing on personal narrative, the author gathers information from various studies and experts in cognitive development. He concludes that babies and young children are talking less due to overuse of technology. Part of talking less means that children are no longer talking to themselves, which is an essential part of identity development. Children who do not talk to themselves are not comfortable with being alone, presumably because they find it more difficult to establish an identity separate from their caregiver.

The second article I found offered more of a scientific approach. "The Impact of Background Television on Parent-Child Interaction," from the journal *Child Development*, made use of a lab study to investigate the effect of background television noise in parent/child interactions.[2] The authors of this article suggest that such disruptive technology not only reduces the quality and quantity of interaction between the child and parent but also that this in turn leads to language delays. In the study, infants who were exposed to background television noise not only interacted less with their parents but had lower-quality interactions as well when compared to infants who did not have the distraction of a television in the background.

After reading these articles, I reflected more deeply on my past observations concerning babies and their use of technology. Every time I attended a party where young children were present, I recalled witnessing a child enjoying an adult's phone or iPad.

These kids were so absorbed in the technology that they did not seem to have any desire to run around and play with each other as I fondly remember doing in my childhood.

Despite growing up in the era of technology domination, I find it troubling to watch a group of children sitting together on a couch staring at their electronic devices instead of talking and giggling with each other.

But infants and young children are not the only ones being affected by the overuse of technology. Technology domination among Gen Z teens is rampant. At the lunch table in my high school, I have noticed a dramatic decline in verbal communication when compared to lunches from my middle school years. Teens are using smartphones for games, texting, browsing the web, etc., and this kind of activity has taken over what used to be quality social time at the lunch table. Playing a game with or against each other, whether it is a video game or a word game, is often the extent of interaction between two students.

One of my teachers recently shared with me that she has to confiscate cell phones at an exponential rate compared to just a few years ago. According to her, student addiction to smartphones and other portable technology such as tablet PCs and smartwatches is becoming a major distraction for both teachers and students. Students, for instance, are "tuning out" the lessons, and teachers are subsequently focused on catching students who are looking at their phones. Teachers, she stated, feel that the concepts they are teaching have to compete for attention with the latest updates on social media. From her perspective, addiction to technology is almost as detrimental to learning as addiction to drugs, when the bodily craving becomes unquenchable. The mental distractions caused by technology parallel the physical distractions caused by drugs.

Because of this pervasive use of technology in my generation, I have often heard it said that we are going to become a generation of idiots. Some are concerned that dependence on technology will impact our ability to acquire life skills that play an important part in the development of our identities and our understanding of where we fit within society. According to this argument, skills such as using a map, basic math, how to address someone with a conflicting viewpoint, or knowing how to generate excitement or enthusiasm are skills that are losing ground in my generation.

Here is a rebuttal perspective from my peers and others who subscribe to the new-world thinking: Why should we consider living life without technology's enhancements? Sure, we are giving up certain skills, just as our ancestors once gave up horseback riding in order to learn how to drive a car. So instead of merely being concerned about skills that are lost, should we not also consider alternative skills that we will develop? Take math skills, for instance: If a calculator can solve an equation for us, does that not free up our minds to ponder new and different methods of mathematical thinking? If we can use an astronomy phone app to identify all the current constellation positions, could that not free up our minds to inquire into what lies beyond in the universe? After all, it is the human mind and generations of hard work that led to today's technological inventions. Why should we assume we will become lazy and no longer progress technologically?

Both of these perspectives seem to be extreme ends of the same spectrum—the technology spectrum. And in such cases, the answer often lies somewhere in the middle. We must acknowledge that the pace of technological advancement has continued to accelerate over the span of generations. So it would be foolish not to take advantage of these advancements to improve the quality of our lives, just as we take advantage of medical enhancements to improve our health. For instance, it would be absurd to use a Rolodex to retrieve a phone number instead of storing such information in our smartphones. Similarly, it would be illogical to avoid using a calculator for a math problem if the calculator can perform the task. But, on the other hand, it should be used only after an individual has proven his ability in performing that same math problem on paper, and thereby demonstrated his ability at acquiring the critical processing necessary for such a task.

In other words, with the adoption of new technology, we often become so blinded by the positive enhancements that we do not always bother to consider the unintended consequences, whether to our own lives or to others. For example, our dependence on digital games for recreation and the influence of social media on our identity are unlike anything that previous generations have encountered. In shifting certain social, communication, and life skills to our digital devices, we are losing certain abilities that form the basis of who we are, what we think, what we perceive, how we make the decisions we make, and ultimately the actions we carry out. Even toddlers are exhibiting delayed speech and an inability to relate to themselves, which form the basis for identity development. These trends could impart language and relationship barriers upon future generations that will undoubtedly affect society as a whole.

Moreover, while one's personal identity can evolve over time, one's online persona often does not, or at least not within the individual's control. This can lead to a divergence between our real identity and our online persona; such a divergence is often the basis for a full-blown identity crisis. In resolving the crisis, many seek to remove or modify their online information. Yet we are learning that what exists online today may exist online forever.

To illustrate, one of my good friends recently had a job interview at a local pizzeria. She was confident that she would get the job. During the interview, the store manager relayed his negative experience with previous employees, citing examples of former workers who would give away free pizza to their friends or who would show up late to work. *I'm not like those workers*, she thought. *I'll get this job and prove just how good I am.* As she was about to share her thoughts, the store manager pulled up her online social media pictures, tags, and other postings. Suddenly my friend realized that she had been judged before she had even met the manager in person. The manager had seen pictures of her playing pranks on her friends, complaining about her previous job, and criticizing one of her teachers. What she thought were innocent moments shared with her friends now led to a perception of her as someone who was immature and naïve.

Although she could not deny these incidents, she took the opportunity to explain herself and the events in a different light. The interview continued for another thirty minutes. My friend left feeling confident that she had clarified the misperception of her character based on her online persona. Alas, three days later, she got a call telling her that the position had been filled. Her online postings had cost her the job opportunity. The lessons to be learned: With each online action we take a potentially permanent digital step and make a potentially public statement. With each such action is formed an unknown digital footprint that could soon be uncovered and come back to haunt us. It is always wise to use caution, no matter what you are posting or with whom you may think you are sharing information.

Notes

1. Nick Bilton, "The Child, the Tablet and the Developing Mind," *New York Times*, March 31, 2013, http://bits.blogs.nytimes .com/2013/03/31/disruptions-what-does-a-tablet-do-to-the -childs-mind.

2. H. L. Kirkorian, T. A. Pempek, L. A. Murphy, M. E. Schmidt, and D. R. Anderson, "The Impact of Background Television on Parent-Child Interaction," *Child Development* 80, no. 5 (2009): 1350–59, doi:10.1111/j.1467-8624.2009.01337.x.

Chapter 2

The Digital Footprint

Digital Footprint:

The digital trail, whether seen as good or bad, left behind after any electronically performed action.

Recently my English teacher showed our class a stunning video. It was a short clip that displayed the effects of our digital footprint.[1] In this video, a man sat inside a tent on a street corner (let us call him the "magician"). He would select a random person picked off the street to enter his tent, which was draped in white panels. The person was asked to sit across a desk from the magician, who then asked the stranger some fairly simple questions such as the stranger's name, age, address, family background, interests, and other typical questions one may ask when meeting someone for the first time. After obtaining these answers, the magician would then reveal the stranger's social security number, bank accounts, details of their friendships, the number of children they had, who they were dating, where they had lived and traveled, and many other shockingly personal details.

Not surprisingly, the individuals being interviewed were perplexed, amazed, and clearly taken aback by this experience. After overcoming some of their emotions (they were obviously still in awe but beginning to get past it), these participants conveyed the "how did you know?" look to the magician. The magician did not respond verbally but rather abruptly dropped the surrounding curtains, revealing a stunning setup of thousands of dollars' worth of computer equipment. Each computer was operated by a member of the magician's team. As is obvious when the panels drop, the magician's team members were conducting extensive online research based on the answers provided by the individual.

Simple facts about a person's life (such as name, address, and occupation) can reveal a wealth of information online and thus reveal a significant portion of one's identity.

I was astonished and anxious after watching this video. I always knew that we leave behind a digital footprint when we place any information online. I knew that in many cases, it is impossible to permanently delete the information after it has been uploaded. But after watching this video, I realized that I did not appreciate the degree to which this information can be accumulated and stored in cyberspace, ready to be pulled up or even hacked into at any moment.

What does privacy really mean in the online world? I wondered. It was a scary thought to know that there is information about myself that others are able to access without my knowledge. I wondered who "out there" might have gleaned my personal details—a feeling not unlike being stalked. After watching this video, I became acutely aware of my digital footprint. *But how did I create this?* I pondered, and in hindsight my tracks revealed the answer: we give out unnecessary information to almost every website we visit, starting with the search engine within our browser. Because of the zeal we possess when we click on our browsers, we do not stop and think about the information we are giving away. On many websites, we answer every question, even if it is not necessary, simply to move to the next button. We are always eager to arrive at the "submit" button, glancing past the "I agree" fields.

The amount of information collected by social media sites is bewildering. While we as users are so caught up in fostering, promoting, or manipulating relationships online, we are oblivious to the information being gathered about us. Clearly, social media is often an effective way to arrange time together, congratulate one another on achievements, and enjoy each other's happy moments. It allows for friends and family, both nearby and distant, to keep up with the latest details in each other's lives. Social media can even maintain relationships by providing a quick way to connect when there is insufficient time for verbal communication.

Moreover, from a professional standpoint, social media has become the de facto method to get one's name "out there." In the current era, for example, a potential employer will run an Internet search on a possible job candidate. The prospective employer will then look up the job candidate on multiple social media websites. If the employer cannot find anything on the job candidate (such as education, previous work experience, or group affiliations)—or if what the employer finds is less than flattering—then a shadow may be cast over the candidate. So in a sense, social media can be viewed as a necessity in contemporary society. Our online life is a double-edged sword that we need to use carefully.

But does that mean we cannot approach social media in a more conscious and cautious fashion? Because we have already concluded that social media and our participation in the digital world are essential to contemporary life, we cannot disregard the idea of social media altogether. On the other hand, we can say that a more cautious approach is necessary. For instance, many social media websites have various features that allow users to keep specific information private. This information, not viewable to the public or to your entire contact group, is—in theory—protected. Although the actual website and company have access to it, other individuals do not. But for some reason, many users neglect this idea of keeping some information private. Many display cell phone numbers, addresses, family member's names, etc., on social media websites for the eyes of the public. What strikes me the most is that information that can obviously be kept private is being shared regardless. This is what I mean by taking a more conscientious approach.

Social media is, in a way, becoming the foundation to our society, but we must understand the responsibilities that come along with "signing in." Hurried individuals miss the fact that random strangers might view personal information that can and should be kept private. With participation must come protection. Simple steps like reading the "Terms and Conditions" clauses may prove helpful. To illustrate, recently I was offered a "free vacation" prize—but in order to accept it, I had to agree that my information could be shared with other vacation-related organizations. As I examined the fine print, I noticed that I would also be authorizing for my information to be disseminated to banks, hotel chains, airline agencies, and car rental services.

Here is another example depicting the unexpected consequences of our online activity. When I received my first iPhone, I noticed a section called "Location Services" under the settings menu. I clicked on this section, and what I discovered was rather astonishing. It was a listing of various apps that were automatically programmed to enable the discovery of my exact location. The Facebook app, for instance, would share my location every time I uploaded a picture. I understand that many of us might add a caption sharing our general location—however, with this setting turned on, after just a few clicks through the picture, one could find my exact geographical grid, and thus I would be "geotagged."[2] Anyone could discover where I was standing without my ever mentioning it. They would know my exact longitude and latitude. Scary!

There is a website called www.ICanStalkU.com. Ben Jackson, one of the site's cofounders, uses this website as a means to educate the public about how easy it is to know where someone is and how that information could be used for malicious intent. He explains that if a couple were to post a picture of their newly acquired flat screen TV and then later post another picture of themselves out of the house, a criminal could check the geotag of the latest picture and determine how far the couple is from their house. The criminal could then decide if that gave him enough time to steal the flat screen while they were still out. The criminal could formulate a plan while sitting at his house. How convenient for him.[3]

This is just one hypothetical scenario, but cases of criminals following a person's online "bread crumbs" have unfortunately happened numerous times in the past.

Although a geotag is presumably meant for convenience (say, for instance, you wanted to know when and where you took a vacation photo), it has an obvious negative and unexpected side effect. Your safety could be compromised all by the simple posting of a picture. But if you are being conscientious about your digital footprint, then perhaps you might post vacation pictures after you return home from vacation instead of while still on vacation. This will ensure that no one can glance at your profile and know that your house is empty.

The information that Ben Jackson from www.ICanStalkU .com can find in a few minutes is much less compared to the extensive work done by the magician in my first example. However, it does make it clear that the average individual could access enough information to theoretically pull off a successful robbery or perhaps a kidnapping. Imagine if the parents of a child went out to a party an hour away and posted a picture of themselves at the event. Imagine if a predator saw this, interpreted the geotag, and knew he could kidnap the child left alone at home. Just imagine. What if the child were you? What if someone knew your daily schedule because of your previously posted pictures? Do you feel as safe as you thought you were?

It is essential for one to be knowledgeable about the degree of one's digital footprint in order to prevent a loss of one's identity—better known as identity theft. One common tactic with identity theft is when someone steals personal information that has been stored in the cloud. The cloud is the network of servers that allow for centralized data storage. It is basically a synonym for the Internet. Instead of using a computer's hard drive, you can store data online in the cloud, which allows you to access information on an indefinite amount of devices. Yahoo!, Google, Dropbox, and Netflix are all popular web-based companies that rely on the cloud. However, for now, one example of the cloud I want to explore more deeply is Apple's iCloud. Let me tell you how I first learned about it.

One day, I was reading my e-mail on my iPhone. I kept getting distracted by various reminders that continually popped up on my screen. They seemed to be reminders about my dad's work and his surgery schedule, so I did not understand why I kept receiving notifications that applied only to my dad. I opened my reminders application and deleted all the irrelevant reminders about his schedule from my phone. I figured no harm would be done since these notifications only amounted to unnecessary distractions on my phone. But I was wrong. Extremely wrong.

What actually occurred was entirely different from what I had expected. In deleting all these reminders from my phone, I also trashed them from my dad's phone. I had no idea how this happened until I realized iCloud was to blame. I had heard of iCloud and thought I fully understood the concept, but, unfortunately, that was not the case. So once I found out iCloud had played a huge role in my mistake, I went to do some research about it.

What I discovered was that iCloud is an intricate system that linked all of our family's iPhones under one account. Therefore, when I deleted my dad's reminders from my phone, I did not realize they would be also deleted from my dad's phone. This led to many complications in my dad's work, and he got frustrated at both the situation and with me.

Now imagine storing information more significant than a personal schedule on iCloud. Vendors have marketed the iCloud as a whole new storage option that avoids tying up local computer space and other backup issues. People now store their home financial information, photographs, videos, and other valuable information on the cloud, which promises to keep your data safe with the security of encryption. Companies such as health care providers keep patient data and image files backed up on the cloud to avoid warehousing huge data files locally. Although it comes with a cost, the promise of safe storage and the reduced investment in hardware has led many to use the cloud for much more than sharing calendars and music.

But suddenly, we are exposed to cyber-terrorism and security breaches on a whole different level. News stories of major retailers getting hacked, resulting in the loss of millions of credit card numbers, are all too commonplace. According to the Identity Theft Resource Center, over three hundred major data breaches occur each year, with highly coordinated and highly sophisticated attempts increasing in number each year.

Companies that specialize in securing confidential data have also become vulnerable, including the Pentagon and the US military. One of the fastest-growing areas of identity fraud is medical identity theft, in which one's insurance information may be sold on the black market to someone else in order to access medical care illegally.[4]

Are there solutions to these extraordinary cases of cyber attacks that have cost the economy billions of dollars a year? Yes, there are a number of solutions, but human nature is one of the biggest forces of resistance. In one study, a group of one hundred and fifty students at the University of Buffalo were followed to determine if they would be susceptible to a typical phishing scam, including one containing grammatical errors and other red flags. What the study found was that the more regularly a student used Facebook, the more likely he or she was to fall for the scam. It seems that our desire to be trusting and pleasing to others can also be our downfall when exposing our identity to others.[5]

Another hurdle to solving the issue of online identity theft is our desire to keep things simple with regard to the amount of time we spend. For instance, data loss is significantly less likely when a solution called *two-factor authorization* is used. In this process, an online user must verify his or her online identity through another mechanism such as a code sent via text to a cell phone number.[6] However, as a society, we usually are not willing to incorporate the cost of these additional steps. But just as we are willing to accept more intense security checkpoints at airports following attacks on our national security, so should we also be willing to consider two-factor authorization in the future as routine if online data breaches continue to result in increasingly greater loss of time and money and higher aggravation.

All of these cases clearly show that our digital footprint can cast a negative shadow over us and impact our ability to function in society. Yet despite red flags that may show up when we communicate online and simple steps that we can take to protect our online information, the vast majority of us remain quite susceptible to a cyber attack. How can we reverse this trend and take back control of our online identities?

First, well-established institutions on the Internet must treat information that is shared more seriously when it relates to identity protection. For many of these companies, their ability to make a profit is based on easy-to-exchange identity platforms. Yet we as the public must demand additional safety measures, especially when teenagers and minors in general are involved. If a teenager is not deemed mature enough to make a choice such as voting in elections, should a teenager be allowed to make choices when it comes to how much information should be shared online? Or should there be some basic regulations that require parental approval in these cases?

Our participation in social media and the digital world has become ever so demanding. Although our digital footprint can prove legitimacy, it can compromise safety. In addition to those effects, social media is becoming a substantial factor in how we are perceived by others, whether by friends, family, employers, or colleagues. Since we are now judged electronically just as we are in person, our identity is increasingly associated with the information we post online.

Notes

1. "Amazing mind reader reveals his 'gift,'" YouTube video, 2:28, from Febelfin, posted by "Duval Guillaume," September 24, 2012, http://www.youtube.com/watch?v=F7pYHN9iC9I.

2. United States Army, *Geotags and Location-Based Social Networking*, accessed August 28, 2014, https://dmna.ny.gov/members /geotagging.pdf.

3. "Dangers of Geotagging," YouTube video, 4:46, from a broadcast by Fox News on January 19, 2011, posted by "SuperUtils Software," March 5, 2011, https://www.youtube.com /watch?v=li8UCrQvgOk.

4. Martyn Williams, "The 5 Biggest Data Breaches of 2014 (So Far)," *PC World*, July 11, 2014, http://www.pcworld.com /article/2453400/the-biggest-data-breaches-of-2014-so-far.html.

5. Arun Vishwanath, "Habitual Facebook Use and Its Impact on Getting Deceived on Social Media," *Journal of Computer-Mediated Communication* 20, no. 1 (2015): 83–98, doi:10.1111 /jcc4.12100.6.

6. Ed Bott, "How to Use an Authenticator App to Improve Your Online Security," *The Ed Bott Report* (blog), ZDNet, November 21, 2014, http://www.zdnet.com/how-to-use-an-authenticator-app -to-improve-your-online-security-7000036049.

Chapter 3

The Offline Identity
in the Online Era

The long-term impact of a digital footprint is receiving greater attention by Generation Z. Teens are becoming savvier with the online trail they leave behind and how it might be perceived by others. Recently, admissions staff at Morehouse College in Atlanta noticed a sharp decline in applicants who used e-mail addresses that contained potentially offensive terms.[1] A popular test prep company also reported a drop in the number of students posting material online that could negatively impact their college admission status.[2]

The European Union has taken this cautionary awareness one step further by establishing an individual's "right to data protection."[3] This law gives any individual living in the European Union the right to remove potentially damaging information from online search engines. In fact, the EU even recommended that the right to data protection—also referred to as "the right to be forgotten"—should be available worldwide.[4] The initiative the EU has taken with online privacy rights is currently far ahead of what we are capable of exercising in the US, where "free speech" arguments must often balance any request to remove potentially damaging information. However, these issues are gaining more attention in the US as well, where the boundaries of what can be posted online are still evolving. In fact, the US Supreme Court may soon decide the limits of what you can post online as it takes on its first case involving free speech and social media.[5]

As the importance of protecting online information becomes a topic of discussion even among teens, it is no wonder that more and more of my friends are returning to a mode of sharing information, thoughts, and feelings face-to-face. But what is interesting about face-to-face communication in the era of texting is that we still tend to avoid topics that might be seen as confrontational or uncomfortable. *Why talk to her about something unpleasant if I could just text her later?* seems to be a common way to think. After all, it might be easier to text an emoticon than to share an emotion in person.

I have witnessed this approach advance to the next level, in which individuals prefer to spend their time only with others who have similar beliefs, where they are less likely to encounter the challenge of opposing views. Here again, the online world simplifies the work to find others with similar interests and views, to the point that engaging with a neighbor who may have different views requires more effort. If I want to find others who are unhappy with the local city government, I can go online and join a group sharing similar views. If I want to prevent the building of a shopping megaplex in my neighborhood, I can find a group that will support my view (just as easily as I can find a local group that takes the opposite stance). These examples illustrate how powerfully the online information we obtain influences the offline choices we make. No matter how diverse our community is, it can still become a "small world" if we continue to gravitate toward like-minded people.

Online or offline, identity is an issue that plagues teens into their twenties. Sometimes it is easier to establish an online identity because it can be created and molded swiftly with your imagination. We find it easier to exercise our creativity when we have backspace and delete keys. Offline, we are now seen for who we are. We are judged by the groups we belong to, the sports we play, the clothing we wear, the words we speak, and sometimes our posture. When learning to interview, we are even taught how to do a proper, confident handshake. Every movement can be judged.

Moreover, every activity we partake in can shape our perceived identity. Imagine two athletes, one a football player and one a tennis player. Which athlete would you suspect to be stronger? Might you assume the tennis player is smarter than the football player? Of the two, who would you conclude to be faster? Stereotypes tag along with the various groups with which we associate ourselves. Our offline identity is shaped not only by the people we hang out with but also by the way others view these groups.

To illustrate, I will share a personal story about a summer course I attended at Duke University. It was a three-week session called "Duke TIP Summer Studies."[6] I attended this course without knowing anyone else who would attend; therefore, my identity could be remade from scratch. During the first week, I approached other kids who I found to be athletic, outgoing, or funny. Eventually this became the only group of people I spent time with. By limiting myself to this group, I did not meet anyone with other personality traits. However, one day toward the end of the session, I met a kid—let us call him David—with whom I had not spoken during these three weeks. He was sitting next to me under a tree as we were both trying to escape the summer heat.

Since I presumed he was sitting under the tree for the same reason as I was, I figured mentioning the weather would be a good conversation starter. I looked at him and said, "It's pretty hot out, isn't it?" David did not look back at me but rather continued to look ahead as he said, "Yeah, I guess." I was puzzled at his manner of responding because it felt like he was ignoring me. So I kept quiet and turned my head in the other direction. Moments later, David turned to me and said, "Sorry for that; I'm just not used to talking to people like you." He introduced himself and asked me for my name. I glanced over at him and saw that he had turned his head, stuck out his hand for a handshake, and spoke more genuinely. I replied by telling him my name, but I was somewhat perplexed at his comment. *What was that supposed to mean: "people like you"? Was that an insult?* I thought.

"That's a cool name," said David. I asked him what he meant when he said he did not talk to people like me. He told me that he thought I was a jock. He said he assumed I would be an arrogant person, the type that laughed at kids like him. I was dumbfounded by this comment. How could he have this absurd perception of me? I was just meeting this guy for the first time.

Then I thought back over the facts that might have led to his conjecture. I concluded that his assumptions came from the group that I had been associating with—a group of kids I had chosen to be around based on their having traits I perceived to be "cool." But during the entire time that I had spent with the "cool" kids, I was being perceived by others as conceited. I was merely trying to associate myself with similar athletic individuals, but stereotypes affected my persona.

At this summer camp, arrogance and hubris were the terms classifying the group of students with whom I had associated myself.

I tried not to let the comment bother me and carried on a normal conversation with David. Somehow, maybe ten minutes into our discussion, we entered the realm of "deep thoughts" for teenagers—we discussed religion, the universe, and the creation of mankind. After about forty-five minutes, David made an interesting comment: "You're kinda like a coin. You've got two personalities. Your tails side is your sporty way of being, and your heads side is your deep, meaningful, conversational way of being." He smiled, said, "Nice to meet you," and left.

As I contemplated David's comment further, I had a eureka moment; I saw how others' perspectives shape how we construct our identities. I may identify myself as a congenial person, but someone else may identify me as aloof. Both perspectives influence my identity as well as my persona.

Even when we pass someone or barely talk to someone, we automatically attribute characteristics to this person. We don't get to truly understand who they are, but we quickly pass judgment. Take, for instance, the first day of school. You sit in class. You look up and see someone you have never met walk through the door. They walk over to their seat and plop down. In those few seconds, you have convinced yourself that you know everything about that person. You tell yourself that you don't need to know who they are because you have already figured it out. We are all guilty of this.

I believe this phenomenon, while always present, is worsening in the digital era, where we do not have the same standard of interaction as mankind did in previous eras. Nowadays, we want to avoid the painstaking process of actually getting to know an individual. Why go through all that hard work if we can figure out who a person is in a matter of seconds with the help of online resources? We have rid ourselves of the old ways of communication: the mode in which someone would approach an individual, talk to him or her, and identify with that person based on an actual conversation. Now, with communication focused on digital forms, the desire to talk to someone face-to-face for the first time can seem like a weary, burdensome activity. It could be inconvenient, awkward, and just not preferable.

Although I firmly believe ridding ourselves of all judgment is virtually impossible, I do believe the amount of labeling to which we subject each other can be reduced. Instead of making it a conscious decision to stereotype someone, we could, instead, just meet the person. But this is becoming less natural, and I believe that is why society tends to create an environment in which we place more emphasis on how we should come across rather than attempt to convey who we actually are. Instead of trying to *eliminate* quick labels or first impressions, we are now taught how to *change* quick labels applied to us. For example, we are taught how to shake a person's hand since that action in itself can create judgment. So we might as well try to make that judgment advantageous to ourselves. It is in this manner that other individuals can affect our offline persona. We change our behavior, and therefore who we are in the moment, to look better. We mold our identities to achieve a positive advantage in the minds of others, who are increasingly likely to judge us before many real words are exchanged. This is something people have always done, but the digital age allows us in Generation Z to look back over words and actions and reflect upon them. What could we stand to learn?

Notes

1. Natasha Singer, "Toning Down the Tweets Just in Case Colleges Pry," *New York Times*, November 19, 2014, http://www.nytimes .com/2014/11/20/technology/college-applicants-sanitize -online-profiles-as-college-pry.html.

2. Kaplan Test Prep, "Kaplan Test Prep Survey: Percentage of College Admissions Officers Who Visit Applicants' Social Networking Pages Continues to Grow—But Most Students Shrug," news release, November 20, 2014, http://press.kaptest.com/press -releases/kaplan-test-prep-survey-percentage-of-college -admissions-officers-who-visit-applicants-social-networking-pages -continues-to-grow-but-most-students-shrug.

3. European Commission, *Factsheet on the "Right to be Forgotten" Ruling (c-131/12)*, 2014, http://ec.europa.eu/justice/data -protection/files/factsheets/factsheet_data_protection_en.pdf.

4. Article 29 Data Protection Working Party, "Adoption of Guidelines on the Implementation of the CJEU's Judgement on the 'Right to be Forgotten,'" news release, November 26, 2014, http:// ec.europa.eu/justice/data-protection/article-29/press-material /press-release/art29_press_material/20141126_wp29_press _release_ecj_de-listing.pdf.

5. Lyle Denniston, "Argument Analysis: Taking Ownership of an Internet Rant," *SCOTUSblog*, December 1, 2014, http://www .scotusblog.com/2014/12/argument-analysis-taking-ownership -of-an-internet-rant.

6. Duke University Talent Identification Program, http://tip.duke.edu /node/11.

Your living is determined not so much by what life brings to you as by the attitude you bring to life; not so much by what happens to you as by the way your mind looks at what happens.

—*Unknown*

Part 2

Attitudes

Should smoking be banned in all public places? Is euthanasia justifiable? Should background checks be necessary for those who want to purchase a gun? What is your opinion of the death penalty?

Whether or not you can passionately argue for one side or the other is not the point. What is important is the fact that you likely have opinions on these issues. Your opinions, in turn, arise from your beliefs and values, which are deeply linked to your identity. These deeply held beliefs and values are what I refer to as your attitudes. Attitude is a word that we hear daily, but like many other words in the English language, attitude has more than one meaning. We are typically used to hearing the word attitude in phrases such as "Have a good attitude!" or "Watch your attitude, mister" or "I don't have an attitude; I'm just tired." In these common expressions, the word attitude is used loosely and refers to one's behavior and present mood. But I want to explore a deeper aspect of the word.

I want to explore the underlying, driving forces behind our tendency to react in a certain way. Our emotional reactions, as well as our thoughts and beliefs, influence our behaviors and thus our attitude toward a given topic. Our attitudes can develop both consciously and subconsciously, and they can be rational or irrational. While our personal experiences shape our attitudes, so do our observations of what is happening around us. What we observe with our friends, in our society, or perhaps in the news can have a significant impact on our attitudes.[1]

How exactly do we develop attitudes from the time of birth? Research has shown that children are naturally curious and instinctively equipped to learn through observation and investigations. Every toy, every word, and every experience has a deep impact on the child's understanding of the world. "Learning changes the brain because it can rewire itself with each new stimulation, experience, and behavior," says Eric Jensen, author of *Teaching with the Brain in Mind*.[2] A child's brain is constantly looking for patterns; each time a child repeats a skill or a task, that pattern is reinforced. The more a pattern is reinforced, the more those neural pathways are strengthened and the harder it is to undo that thought or task being reinforced. Thus, the development of an attitude is associated with the very basis of learning and thought. And while attitudes can be controlled and modified over time, the more that attitudes are reinforced, the harder those attitudes are to change.

As a teenager, I can better appreciate the role that parents and family have played in shaping my attitudes than I possibly could have as a child. However, I am also aware of the speed at which news and information travel in my generation and thus mindful of the increasingly greater impact that society and external factors have in shaping the attitudes of Generation Z. Of these external factors, I will explore three influences that I believe strongly impact Gen Z attitudes: the impact of corporate America and the economy, the impact of changing cultural values, and the impact of social media and other technology platforms as they provide rapid feedback on the choices we make.

First, let us start with examining the impact of the corporate American ideology. Every day, whether it takes place through a TV commercial, someone speaking on the radio, a magazine, an article, or a billboard, we are exposed to some sort of advertisement. These advertisements are cleverly constructed to persuade us to buy a product. The entire point of an advertisement, from a business perspective, is to provide the consumer a good attitude and a positive vibe toward a product. In order to achieve this goal, businesses attempt to psychologically manipulate the consumer into believing that the product has many pros and minimal, if any at all, cons. To do this, businesses use a psychological term called *classical conditioning*. Classical conditioning is the act of pairing two separate stimuli. Beer companies do a great job of this.

Typically, when we see a beer commercial on television, it portrays beer as a product that allows you to relax. In the commercial, a group of people may be on the beach, drinking some beer and simply having fun, of course while being responsible. The goal of this type of commercial is to associate the consumer's idea of relaxation with the company's beer—the pairing of two separate stimuli. This method of advertising shapes our attitude toward the product. Throughout our life, our attitudes toward a countless number of products have been shaped subconsciously. This is the manner in which businesses play a major role in shaping our perceptions.

Corporations have also invested extensively in understanding the psychology of decision making, of enjoyment, and of how to create a positive attitude. Even the roles that music and smell play in luring shoppers to a store and changing a customer's attitudes toward a brand have been studied extensively. All this is evidence that creating brand loyalty is not necessarily about a better-quality product or a related tangible benefit, but rather about creating a positive attitude toward the product or service. Businesses often conduct research and employ consultants whose exclusive role is to change your attitude. The use of music, fragrances, and even values or institutions that Americans hold dear (such as loyalty to the US Constitution and the Bill of Rights) have all been incorporated to shape our attitudes. One of the most classic companies with expertise in this area is Coca-Cola, which has been able to link the drinking of Coke products with family bonding, friendship, laughter, security, and happiness for generations. Coke's advertisement platform known as "I'd like to buy the world a Coke and keep it company" is considered one of the world's greatest commercials at evoking these emotions.[3]

The influence of corporate America in shaping teenage Gen Z attitudes cannot be underestimated. The extent to which we have become comfortable with letting corporate agendas infiltrate our everyday life is remarkable. Take, for instance, Channel One, a news and educational television channel marketed to schools. Despite the fact that this TV channel relied on corporate advertising to make the availability of this service feasible, schools instead focused on the educational content offered. The irony of this situation, however, was brought to light by none other than the American Academy of Pediatrics, which reported in their official journal a study concluding that children watching Channel One remembered the commercials better than they did the news and educational information.[4]

In addition to businesses, the role of the economy—and specifically the role of the Great Recession of 2007 to 2009—has most certainly influenced the attitudes of Gen Z. Growing up hearing that companies worth billions of dollars can suddenly go broke overnight is enough to rattle anyone, even teens. I recall hearing about *subprime mortgages* well before I knew what the term actually meant. I knew enough, though, to know that they wreaked havoc on the economy. I also knew that pension plans provided workers with financial security after retirement but that these benefits were fast eroding. I grew up hearing my grandparents talking about how they have worked for the same company for decades but knew that no one expects to do so any longer. When we have no guarantee that being a pleasant, hard worker will provide us long-term job security and no guarantee that even a billion-dollar company is stable, our desire for greater control and increased opportunities for entrepreneurship shape our economic attitudes.

Along with corporate America and the economy, our cultural values are also influencing our attitudes. For example, the relationship between parents and children is changing. Although many think there is a disconnect between parents and their children, I believe that what we are actually experiencing is a general disconnect among people due to our over-reliance on technology as a substitute for conventional relationships. While children and parents of my generation may not communicate in the same manner as generations before—for example, talking during car rides or around a dinner table—I believe that overall communication through different modalities is the same, if not improved. Statistics by Nickelodeon support this. In a study published in 2012, sixty-nine hundred children who are members of Gen Z as well as eighty-seven hundred parents of Gen Z children participated in an online survey that spanned eleven countries. The results showed that two-thirds of parents believe they are closer to their children than their parents were to them. In addition, 83 percent of parents consider their child to be one of their best friends.[5] Obviously, these changing relationships affect Gen Z attitudes in many ways.

Another change in cultural trends is our awareness that collaborative forces can make a difference socially, environmentally, and even politically. For instance, we have seen the fall of political regimes accelerated by social media. In 2011, the citizens of Egypt used various social media websites to organize campaigns and protest demonstrations and to protest government action via comments on government Facebook sites such as the Egyptian Armed Forces page. After the outbreak of confrontational comments on Facebook, a government official actually closed comments sections on various Facebook sites. To keep the discussion going, the activists used Twitter and popularized the hashtag #nomiltrials. Salma el Daly, an Egyptian video blogger, said, "Twitter and Facebook are the ways we keep the momentum going. We protect and defend people. We campaign there."[6]

Even attitudes toward self-destructive behaviors have improved in my generation. Take smoking, for instance. The latest "Monitoring the Future" survey funded by the National Institute on Drug Abuse finds that teens and young adults are smoking fewer cigarettes, drinking less alcohol, and abusing fewer prescription and synthetic drugs. There has also been a sharp drop in binge drinking among high school seniors, now under 20 percent, compared to 1998, when binge drinking among high school seniors was at a peak of 31.5 percent.[7]

Let us not forget the impact technology and social media have on shaping Gen Z attitudes by influencing the choices we make. I believe our personal experiences are the leading factors that shape our perceptions and attitudes in life because every second of our life, we are doing something. Our body never stops functioning and processing information from birth until death. This means that every second, we have an opportunity to learn something new. Every second in our life contains the opportunity to shape our attitudes. Risk taking, experiences with authority, and acts of experimentation are all life experiences that greatly affect our values and attitudes, and they are also highly influenced by social media.

Throughout our lives, we encounter risks. How late we stay up, how we drive, and how we make bets with a friend are all examples of risks we have seen numerous times. But how do these simple risks shape our attitude toward bigger ones? To answer this question, I am going to share a personal story. When I was about seven years old, I made my first bet. I was having dinner at Olive Garden with my family, and our appetizers had just been served. In the middle of the table was a nice basket of warm breadsticks. I picked one up and was about to eat it when my dad stopped me. He took it out of my hands and said, "If I eat this entire breadstick in one bite, you have to give me your room. But if you win, I will give you five dollars." I was amused at such a dumb bet; of course I would win. It seemed like such an easy way to win five dollars (at age seven, that was a lot of money), so of course I agreed. My dad opened his mouth and shoved the entire breadstick into his mouth. He chewed it, swallowed, drank some water, and smiled.

I was speechless. How the heck did my dad do that? He looked at me and said, "So I guess I own your room now!" I begged for my room back, and my dad laughed hysterically. He eventually agreed to give me my room back, but I learned right then that no matter how sure you are that you will win a bet, you can never be certain about the future. That experience shaped my attitude toward all future bets. I have shied away from bets; very rarely do I agree to any. This is a perfect illustration of how a small risk can influence future decisions about risk taking.

Years later, I was introduced to online fantasy sports leagues, where relatively small wagers potentially could win you large sums of money. Despite their similarity to gambling, fantasy sports leagues that reward winners with payouts are exempt from gambling laws and thus have proliferated in the Internet age.[8] My interest in these activities was tempered by my experience with my dad. But then I pondered, *What if I didn't have such an experience to fall back on? What if I had become engrossed by these online fantasy sports sites—and then was tempted to enter online gambling sites?* I realized how easy the Internet has made it to take risks. Other risky behaviors such as bullying, sexting, or threatening violence have been extensively covered in the media after their rapid rise through social media. These examples show how the speed of online communication, with its anonymity and lack of face-to-face interaction, has led to an increase in risk-taking attitudes that Gen Z members need to be aware of as they grow into adulthood.

Experiences with authority are also important life events that shape our attitudes. Since birth, we have looked up toward an authoritative figure. Whether it be by our parents, grandparents, older siblings, police officers, bosses, or our own government, we have been affected by those in positions of influence. The experiences we have with these individuals form our attitude toward authority. Let's say you have always felt that you cannot meet your parents' expectations. Perhaps this led you to think that you are not "good enough." Perhaps this issue has led you to experience lower self-esteem or irritation as you try to please your parents. Or let's say you have issues at school with teachers. You might feel like you are treated unfairly. Perhaps this has led to strong feelings of dislike toward a teacher, which has led you to not follow directions or take orders from someone who does act in a fair manner. If you feel like you should not take orders from your teachers or parents, this mentality will carry forth toward, for instance, police officers. If you believe that authority has treated you unjustly in the past and therefore forfeited the right to demand something from you, then you may feel that police officers are too strict and that following all the laws is a waste of time. You may then have a poor attitude toward police officers simply because you see them as one more person who has power over you. Your experiences with one form of authority will shape your attitude toward other forms of authority.

Gen Z's attitudes toward authority are interesting. On the one hand, we are respectful of our parents and others in positions of power. On the other hand, we are comfortable maintaining casual relationships as we communicate with people in such positions through e-mail, Twitter, and other online platforms. For instance, students are willing to respect rules in a classroom, but then be critical of a teacher online. This tactic could be viewed as far more disrespectful than what may have been intended. To illustrate, one year a few teammates on my basketball team complained online with a sarcastic post, "I love being a benchwarmer!" This post was retweeted many times, eventually reaching the coaches. The coaches viewed this as highly critical of their decision making and strategy. The players were subsequently penalized and became embarrassed. So while my generation believes that those in authority are more approachable, we need to be careful that this attitude is not taken advantage of to the extent that we then become disrespectful toward the same people.

Lastly, acts of experimentation can affect your outlook on learning. When we were infants, we experimented with our world. Ripping paper apart or banging on the table were ways to learn about our surroundings. But what if we were always told to stop doing something? What if we were yelled at for ripping paper up and making a mess? The likelihood is that we probably would have stopped doing it. In fact, we probably quit many methods of experimentation because we were told to stop. How might this shape our attitude toward education? Chances are that if you were the type of child who was always building or experimenting, you have a greater love of learning. But if you were always told to stop experimenting, you may not have as strong a passion for learning. So as early as childhood, our attitudes have been shaped subconsciously. Your attitude toward education could stem from whether or not you were encouraged to experiment with the world when you were a mere infant.

In my generation, online platforms have made collaboration, creativity, and experimentation more available. Social media has made it easier for us to find like-minded people. Websites and online forums allow members to share their experiences and seek feedback on ideas before they become official publications. Crowdfunding sites have made it easier to raise money. Still other sites have made it easier to bring a new product to market with third-party assistance. My generation will benefit heavily from greater experimentation and from our ability to find others who share common ground to help break through obstacles that otherwise would be difficult to surpass.

All of these examples show how our attitudes in life are affected by many external factors. In this section, I have written about how our attitudes toward various topics have been shaped by contemporary stimuli. In chapter 4, I will talk about our generation's attitudes toward finances. In chapter 5, I will address the importance of education and how our attitudes toward education have been formed. In chapter 6, I will address the attitudes teens have toward competition and how our society has shaped us to value winners. Finally, in chapter 7, I will discuss how our political attitudes have been shaped since we were young children and how this will affect our future voting habits.

Notes

1. Gregory R. Maio and Geoff Haddock, *The Psychology of Attitudes and Attitude Change* (Thousand Oaks: Sage Publications, 2009).

2. Eric Jensen, *Teaching with the Brain in Mind* (Alexandria: Association for Supervision & Curriculum Development, 2005).

3. "Animated History of Coca-Cola," YouTube video, 5:30, from commercials by the Coca-Cola Company, posted by "Coca-Cola Conversations," April 13, 2011, https://www.youtube.com/watch?v=Pdrr3ZxZUOc.

4. Erica Weintraub Austin, Yi-Chun "Yvonnes" Chen, Bruce E. Pinkleton, and Jessie Quintero Johnson, "Benefits and Costs of *Channel One* in a Middle School Setting and the Role of Media-Literacy Training," *Pediatrics* 117, no. 3 (March 1, 2006): e423–e433, doi:10.1542/peds.2005-0953.

5. John Consoli, "Nickelodeon Study Affirms Kids' Strong Influence on Family Purchasing Decisions," *Broadcasting & Cable*, August 22, 2012, http://www.broadcastingcable.com/news/news-articles/nickelodeon-study-affirms-kids-strong-influence-family-purchasing-decisions/113500.

6. Tanja Aitamurto, "How Social Media Is Keeping the Egyptian Revolution Alive," *MediaShift* (blog), PBS, September 13, 2011, http://www.pbs.org/mediashift/2011/09/how-social-media-is-keeping-the-egyptian-revolution-alive256.

7. The University of Michigan, "Use of Alcohol, Cigarettes, and a Number of Illicit Drugs Declines among U.S. Teens," news release, December 16, 2014, http://www.monitoringthefuture.org//pressreleases/14drugpr_complete.pdf.

8. Joshua Brustein, "Fantasy Sports and Gambling: Line is Blurred," *New York Times*, March 11, 2013, http://www.nytimes.com/2013/03/12/sports/web-sites-blur-line-between-fantasy-sports-and-gambling.html.

Chapter 4

Developing Financial Awareness

When I was a freshman in high school, my dad and I attended a rock concert together in Dallas. It was my very first concert, so my dad splurged on great seats with access to a private lounge before the show. The whole experience was amazing. There were about fifteen thousand people attending the concert, and the music was roaring. The show included special effects like lasers and fireballs.

Before we took our seats, we visited the special lounge area. Here we relaxed for about an hour with drinks and snacks. There were only about one hundred concertgoers in this section, so my dad and I were able to sit down peacefully on some comfortable couches before we went on to the booming concert. As we left this area to go to our seats, a janitor reservedly asked us how much our tickets had cost. My dad responded by saying that he had spent two hundred dollars total for the two tickets. The janitor sighed and mumbled back, "Wow, that's a lot of money. I wish I could afford tickets to see a concert." My dad flashed an awkward smile, and we walked out the door.

That brief interaction with the janitor as he shared his wish to attend a concert he couldn't afford, despite the fact that he obviously worked hard as a janitor, offered me a new insight to my current experience. Here I was with my dad at a concert with great seats, having drinks and food on comfortable couches in the lounge. Not once had I thought about how luxurious my experience was. Not once had I thought about how much this experience must have cost. Not once had I thought about what the value of a single concert ticket could mean for someone else.

The next day after the concert, as I thought more about what the janitor had shared, I looked around and at once had a sincere appreciation for a number of things that I had taken for granted until that moment. I was appreciative of the fact that I had my own bedroom, lived in a nice city, enjoyed concerts and movies, and attended a high school that had the resources to offer a wide variety of extracurricular activities.

Then I thought about the many friends I had whose mother or father (or both) had lost their jobs. I also recalled several friends whose older siblings had trouble finding jobs after graduating from college and were back home living with their parents. I could think of five high school friends who had after-school jobs like me. But while I had an after-school job with the intention of gaining new skills, several of my friends were working primarily to contribute to family expenses. I also thought of two friends who had to move out of their houses because these families could no longer afford their mortgage payments.

I looked up recent economic trends and began to understand the severity of the impact that the recession that began in 2007 had on both the US and the world economy. It was the most lingering recession since the Great Depression. What

I grew up seeing made more sense now. Despite the fact that many teens in my generation seem spoiled or better off than previous generations due to the fact that we own smartphones, laptops, and other technological gadgets, we are still acutely aware of the impact of world events such as financial disasters and terrorism and how they affect our own lives. In fact, we have used our technological advancements to help us become more exposed to worldly issues and more cognizant of international matters.

It seems that for this reason, a recent study by TD Ameritrade shows that 46 percent of Gen Z teens reported being worried about student debt after college graduation.[1] Based on the Cassandra report, 57 percent of teens would rather save their money than spend it.[2] And a United Nations study found that if a typical member of Gen Z was given five hundred dollars, 70 percent of those surveyed said they would save at least a part of it.

These percentages are a contrast to the previous two generations (Generations X and Y), in which the majority of teens would not save their earnings and would spend their entire current earnings or allowances immediately.[3] Even credit card use has substantially declined in my generation; more than twice as many young adults shunned the use of credit cards in 2012 than had in the seven years prior.[4]

It appears that the economic downturn and the skyrocketing costs of higher education, as well as other factors, have certainly affected my generation's attitude toward money. While we enjoy our interactive, electronic tools, we have come to appreciate the value of financial security and the importance of the economy on our individual lives. However, there is some irony in the fact that many of us are concerned about our current and future financial needs, and it has to do with the fact that so many of us are nonetheless influenced by corporations. We are inundated with corporate brands on a daily basis, and it is no longer solely through television or radio exposure. In fact, most of our exposure is through more targeted approaches, such as sponsored posts on social media or banner ads on mobile devices (and not just in our browser but in our individual apps), via online video services such as YouTube, or even through "sponsored" news stories listed along with regular news on many popular online news sites. The result is that our opinions, as well as our underlying attitudes toward products or services, are being constantly influenced. My generation is influenced by media more than ever before simply because it is exposed to media more than ever before. So it should come as no surprise that in a recent survey by Nickelodeon, over 70 percent of parents ask for their children's opinions when making a purchasing decision, and 28 percent of parents ask for their children's opinions even when the item purchased is exclusively for parental use.[5]

As consumers, my generation has developed an informed and demanding attitude—that is, we know what we want. We understand that life with debt is unsatisfying and has affected our older siblings and parents. We understand that job security is a thing of the past. We know we need to be responsible with money. Being a technologically savvy generation, we know how to research the best price and the best quality. We know how to leave our feedback if we have not had a good experience. And we will share this information with each other through social media. We want to be involved with household business transactions. Although the growing influence of media has allowed for corporations to target us more individually, my generation's technological literacy has allowed us to become more knowledgeable about this issue and therefore more equipped to handle this advertising onslaught.

We know what corporations want, but, more importantly, we know what we want. We welcome the opportunity to let media advertise the various options for us, but we remain confident that we will do the necessary research to make the best decision for us. Contrary to previous generations, who viewed and discounted the media as biased, Gen Z recognizes this form of manipulation as creative education and is able to see through it to ascertain what our reaction should be.

Notes

1. TD Ameritrade IP Company, Inc., *Generation Z and Money Survey 2013,* May 2013, http://www.amtd.com/files/doc _downloads/research/Gen_Z_and_Money_2013_Research _Report_Sept_2013_FINAL.pdf.

2. J. Walter Thompson Company, *Gen Z: Digital in Their DNA,* April 2012, http://www.jwtintelligence.com/trendletters2 /#axzz3Uf9VWFde.

3. Sarah Sladek and Alyx Grabinger, *Gen Z,* February 26, 2014, http://www.slideshare.net/AENC/gen-z-final-white-paper.

4. Frederic Huynh, "The Young and the Cardless," *FICO Blog,* June 10, 2013, http://www.fico.com/en/blogs/risk-compliance/the -young-and-the-cardless.

5. John Consoli, "Nickelodeon Study Affirms Kids' Strong Influence on Family Purchasing Decisions," *Broadcasting & Cable,* August 22, 2012, http://www.broadcastingcable.com/news/news -articles/nickelodeon-study-affirms-kids-strong-influence-family -purchasing-decisions/113500.

Chapter 5

"I Deserve It": Competitive Attitudes in the Era of Entitlement

Generation Z's attitude toward achievement and success is shaped by one major factor: entitlement. I hear it around me all the time: "I should have won" or "I deserved it more than he did." Often, these words are asserted with anger or resentment. Yes, it's pretty obvious that our society values competition but often at the expense of collaboration.

Now, however, the feeling of entitlement further hampers our generation's road to achieving true happiness and success.

I am not implying that we do not appreciate collaboration. In this digital era, I believe my generation collaborates more than any other generation before. We have grown up in a time when it is normal to share and seek a variety of opinions on an issue before we make a decision. We are also comfortable interacting with people of all ages; the Internet and social media have made it easier to do so. We are comfortable sharing our ideas and soliciting feedback from family, friends, and even strangers. In the Internet age, we realize it is also easier to get the attention of a CEO of a company or a government official through e-mail or Twitter. This experience has given us the confidence to collaborate with anyone, in any position, located anywhere in the world.

On the other hand, we have learned from our parents that when jobs are limited and the economy is in a recession, not everyone can be a winner. In this time of uncertainty, retaining a competitive edge has its benefits. In our society, competition is ubiquitous.

Whether we are competing in school sports, for higher academic achievements, or for a promotion at work, we are always striving to do better than our peers. In the past, competition has led to economic growth and technological innovations. Competition allows us to overcome adversity and leap over daunting obstacles. It helps us develop a tenacious attitude, a vital trait in today's world. In our world, success is equated with competition, and competition is associated with winning.

However, competition also implies that if there is a winner, then there is also a loser. For one person to succeed, another has to fail. The notion of winning at any cost is so pervasive in our society that this attitude has overtaken all forms of entertainment.

Turn on the television, and it is clear from the sheer quantity of reality TV shows that everything in life is a competition. The very idea that dancing, singing, and cooking are inherently enjoyable tasks that we may do just for the sheer pleasure of it is replaced with a different attitude—the attitude in which we compete in each of these activities to find the one person who is the best dancer, singer, or cook. The fact that there are multiple reality shows for each of these activities is a reflection of how much competition has taken a foothold in our everyday lives. And we have even taken things beyond these commonplace activities; there are shows about surviving in the wilderness, or worse, surviving in the wilderness *naked*. But why stop there? We can even compete as bachelors or bachelorettes to win an engagement. In these reality shows, there is only one winner, who is often rewarded with a contract in addition to fame and fortune. The rest of the contestants, of course, are losers.

The fact that an activity as subjective as cooking can now be deemed a competitive event is interesting in itself. But this is only the beginning—creative, literary expression such as poetry is now a competitive activity, as made evident by multiple poetry reality shows that are becoming popular around the world.[1] Even the business world is more and more transparent with its "winning is everything" attitude. Businesses often speak in terms of "battling" opponents or of market "domination" and "aggressive" strategies where the goal is to "destroy" the other companies.

Is a competitive society happy? Not when the only measure of success is winning, according to Francesco Duina, author of *Winning: Reflections on an American Obsession*. In this book, Duina makes two interesting observations about the American attitude toward competition and winning. The first is that differentiating between winners and losers allows us to believe that there is equal opportunity for all—but without the need for a social commitment to provide equal benefits to all. Second, Duina points out that in today's society, winning is also about being right; winners are perceived as more credible and thus offered more respect. All aspects of their lives are then considered to be more credible or held to be associated with that winning behavior. Whether the successful person is a celebrity, a professional athlete, a business leader, or a politician, their beliefs and knowledge are given higher regard than their losing rivals.[2]

In another study, "When Less Is More: Counterfactual Thinking and Satisfaction Among Olympic Medalists," an interesting and unexpected fact was discovered about the aftermath of athletic competition. This study, published after the 1992 Olympics, found that those who won bronze medals clearly tended to be happier than the athletes who won silver.[3] The study explored a concept in psychology called *counterfactual thinking*, which describes the human tendency to ponder alternatives to events which have already occurred—in other words, the "what might have been" scenario. The authors of this study attributed their findings to the fact that the silver medalists were internally pondering "what might have been"—if they had won the gold. The bronze medalists, on the other hand, were likely comparing their situation to the scenario of not winning a medal at all.

The issue with "what might have been" reasoning is that it can go down a slippery slope toward the thought of "I should have won." During my summer camp at Duke University, I participated in an Ultimate Frisbee tournament. I had a team of ten players, and we played until the semifinals, where we ended up losing. Many of us were disappointed, especially because we strongly believed we had the capability of winning the entire tournament. After being eliminated, every team member kept complaining and would repeat the same phrase over and over again: "We should have won!"

The more competitive a particular scenario may seem, the more we tend to think this way. In my generation, we also have an appetite for immediate gratification, so the idea that we should try again, try harder, or employ a new strategy for achieving success is not one we often consider. Moreover, most of us have been raised to feel we are always winners—that we always deserve to win. So everyone gets a trophy. This line of reasoning often leads us toward the feeling of entitlement, where we can overestimate our talents and accomplishments or be resistant to honest feedback. We then tend to blame others for our mistakes.

I have noticed that along with a sense of entitlement, we have also developed a fear of trying—because why try my best if I already deserve it? Trying is risky. We tend to think, *If I try my best and fail, that means my best was not good enough.* The fear of trying and the fear of failure go hand in hand. This rationale leads us to believe that if we try hard and fail, we will essentially make fools out of ourselves, especially because an embarrassing loss might convey that subsequent wins are simply "lucky."

In addition to entitlement, we also have a desire to be accepted, to be "cool." Being cool often implies *not* trying your hardest because if you do and fail, then you are seen as a "loser." In my school, we have a name for these kids: the "try-hard" kids. This kind of mentality occurs at my school frequently, and I have noticed it happening around the country as well. When I traveled to California to visit a friend, I heard the term "try-hard" almost daily. Another example occurred when my family went on a cruise. I was watching a youth ping-pong tournament, and those who actually attempted to win were laughed at. These trends keep teens from trying their hardest. Although teens may see this behavior as "cool" for now, it contradicts what we know about our society. We know that our society values the end result. Our society tends to overlook one's path to success and focuses only on the success itself. For instance, we view Oprah Winfrey as a successful woman, yet we overlook the obstacles she has overcome. Oprah was fired from a news TV channel after being told she was "unfit for TV."[4] Michael Jordan, the legendary basketball player, is arguably the best player in history. However, we tend to overlook the fact that he was cut from his high school basketball team.[4] Albert Einstein, the scientific and mathematical genius, was told he did not have the aptitude to complete high school, and in fact dropped out at the age of fifteen.[5] Or there is the example of Walt Disney. He was fired from the *Kansas City Star* because, according to his editor, he "lacked imagination and had no good ideas."[4]

Obviously, these individuals overcame adversity in order to be as respected as they are today. But we often fail to see their struggles; we prefer to see only the successful ending. These examples illustrate the higher emphasis that our society places on the end result and that, for better or for worse, we are willing to overlook the means that have produced that end result. But if we are mindful of this, then why do many teens still worry about how they are perceived, even when they know that the end result is what matters?

I believe some Gen Z teens are not quite mature enough to grasp that being cool in high school is simply a limited form of coolness. It may be cool for now, but apathy in the future won't be cool at all. That is the lesson for my generation to learn as we mature. Success does not come from being passive. Success comes from a burning passion. You must work in order to be successful. If you continue to work hard, success becomes an opportunity. It is never guaranteed, but it becomes a possibility. No matter how many times you fail, continuing to pick yourself back up and work hard will lead to your success. If we place less emphasis on the goal and more emphasis on the path toward that goal, we will build better habits and ultimately achieve more in life.

Notes

1. Chantelle, "Poetry Month 2013: Poetry Reality TV Shows," *Bookkaholic*, April 29, 2013, http://www.bookkaholic.com/poetry-month-2013-poetry-reality-tv-shows.

2. Francesco Duina, *Winning: Reflections on an American Obsession* (Princeton: Princeton University Press, 2010).

3. Victoria H. Medvec, Scott F. Madey, and Thomas Gilovich, "When Less Is More: Counterfactual Thinking and Satisfaction Among Olympic Medalists," *Journal of Personality and Social Psychology* 69, no. 4 (1995): 603–10.

4. Aly Weisman, "15 People Who Failed before Becoming Famous," *Business Insider*, October 29, 2012, http://www.businessinsider.com/15-people-who-failed-before-becoming-famous-2012-10.

5. "Albert Einstein in Brief," *American Institute of Physics*, http://www.aip.org/history/exhibits/einstein/inbrief.htm.

Chapter 6
Learning and Education in the Digital Age

One night, after several hours of mundane, uninspiring homework, I asked myself the question that many students ask: *What's the point of homework?* This might seem like a basic question with obvious answers, but the obvious answers no longer made sense to me. I have been told that homework reinforces concepts that I learn in school. Yet I know that many times, I have completed homework on concepts that were never actually taught in the classroom but which instead were covered in the textbook and which we were therefore expected to know. At other times, I have completed homework on topics that I already fully understood or had previously learned, so the assignment did not add value in terms of my acquiring any new information.

I thought back to a visit I made to my former elementary school. I remember peeking into classrooms and how I could feel the aura of natural curiosity that the children displayed. Yet I also recall how, by middle school, the relationship between teachers and students became more distanced, and at times there was a clear disconnect. While some students did mature and thrive in middle school, many more seemed to lose their natural inquisitiveness. During this time, homework levels increased, but we did not have a clear understanding of why.

At the same time, I noticed that teachers grew increasingly preoccupied by a myriad of district, state, and national test benchmarks. Moreover, their ability to teach toward these testing requirements also became a reflection of the teacher's job performance. So homework, then, was assigned not necessarily to inspire any true learning but rather to ensure that bureaucratic standards were met. Our teacher's goal is that we students are prepared to pass an end-of-year test, many of which are mandated by local or state law.

When I researched the issue further, I discovered two experts on the topic. The first was Gerald LeTendre, Professor of Education at Pennsylvania State University. He concurs that homework often appears to be "a remedial strategy (a consequence of not covering topics in class, exercises for struggling students, a way to supplement poor quality educational settings), and not an advancement strategy (work designed to accelerate, improve, or get students to excel)."[1] The second source I found was a paper published by Stanford that explored an empirical study that found that extensive homework in high school was associated with negative physical symptoms, academic worries, and mental health problems.[2]

But I actually enjoy learning, like many other students. I am fascinated by new discoveries and by learning what kind of work and reasoning went into making those discoveries. Many of my friends and I have spent hours exploring topics that are not taught in school. With ready access to information online, we become our own teachers.

However, as I talked to my classmates and discussed the homework issue through social media, I discovered a general consensus that many high school classes are rigidly structured and inefficient and offer a learning pace designed to follow some sort of mandated timeline. As a result, many teachers do not have time to explore and answer questions on tangential topics that students often ask about.

As I mentioned earlier, humans are inherently curious. So in actuality, all of us should enjoy learning and then implementing these new ideas and skills. The problem seems to be with how students in my generation remain motivated. According to the John W. Gardner Center at Stanford University, there are two types of motivation, intrinsic and extrinsic: "Intrinsic motivation is the natural curiosity and desire to learn that we are all born with. We experience intrinsic motivation when we find ourselves seeking answers to a question that intrigues us or pushing ourselves to work hard to master a skill. Extrinsic motivation is when we work for an external reward or to avoid an external punishment provided by someone else."[3]

Traditionally, we have relied on extrinsic motivation to drive learning, offering rewards such as public acknowledgement, money, the establishment of class rank, or other similar incentives. The theory behind extrinsic motivation was that human behavior could be reinforced in much the same way that animal behavior could be reinforced through the use of treats. However, according to the Gardner Center, more recent research has shown that our intrinsic belief in our ability to be successful has a more significant impact on our motivation to learn. The more we learn through engagement, the greater our intrinsic motivation is to learn, setting up a positive feedback cycle.[4]

More interesting is the fact that extrinsic motivation actually *decreases* our interest and motivation, especially if a student is already inherently motivated to learn, because the motivation shifts from the intrinsic reward to the desire to obtain that extrinsic reward. This happens because that extrinsic reward is felt to be more tangible and because our desire to obtain credit tends to supersede our internal pride and satisfaction at achieving a personal goal. Worse, this shift to extrinsic motivation then creates a competitive atmosphere in learning environments, which in turn creates a whole new set of obstacles toward successful learning. In addition, this focus on extrinsic motivation triggers the attitude of entitlement, the belief that we *deserve* to get a better grade (or better test score) virtually by any means necessary. One consequence of this approach is an extraordinary trend toward grade inflation over the last several decades. There has also been an increased reliance on "curved" test scores such as AP exams, which mask the actual knowledge that students are truly acquiring.[5]

Another factor affecting Gen Z's motivation to learn is the manner in which information is conveyed in classrooms. For instance, we believe learning should be more active and engaging, more fluid, more tangential, and more individualized. In a society in which we have grown used to being able to obtain any level of detail on any topic within seconds, we "tune out" when the whiteboard is full of information that only requires rote memorization because our belief is that we will always have access to that information online. To counter this, we need a learning environment that focuses on the most efficient method to obtain the most accurate information, not necessarily memorizing that information. Growing up in an era where we take high-definition, 3-D graphics for granted, we enjoy visual learning, especially tools that we can manipulate. Yet most classrooms are still primarily designed for passive engagement through a whiteboard or an overhead projector.

An interactive learning experience also promotes a more individualized pace. For example, in my junior year of high school, I was introduced to a website called Membean. This site supports an interactive method for students to learn vocabulary that would have been otherwise taught through rote memorization. As an individual learns a particular set of words at his own pace, the subsequent sets of words grow more complex. This interactive learning style was more successful at enriching our vocabulary than the conventional method. With rote memorization, we may have passed the test, but didn't necessarily incorporate the new vocabulary into our communication or our thoughts. After just a few months of using Membean, many of my peers learned more vocabulary than in the previous two years combined. The use of Membean showcases a broader trend with Gen Z: the use of personal digital technology to study at one's own pace while receiving constant feedback.

In order to create life-long, independent learners, teachers must focus on rekindling that inherent desire to learn in their students. The Gardner Center details specific steps that can rekindle this desire based on current research in psychology and educational theory. I believe that their approach, combined with what we know about Generation Z's attitudes toward engaging, individually paced, visual learning, can dramatically change our current attitude toward learning for the better.

The other significant obstacle affecting our attitude toward learning has to do with the role of competitive attitudes in our educational system. In a previous chapter, I discussed the impact of our competitive attitude in society, but let us further explore the impact of competition on learning and education.

There is good evidence that learning suffers from excessive competition. In his book *No Contest: The Case against Competition*, Alfie Kohn provides a wealth of references on this topic.[6] For example, he cites the research of David and Roger Johnson of the University of Minnesota, which reviewed the results of over one hundred studies between 1924 to 1980. Sixty-five of the studies found that children learn better when they work collaboratively as opposed to competitively, eight found the reverse, and thirty-six found no significant difference. The more complex the learning task, the worse children in a competitive environment fared.

Kohn also cites the research of Robert Helmreich of the University of Texas, which showed that businessmen, scientists, pilots, and other professionals reported that a personal challenge meant more to them than achievement through competition.

Stanford University's "Challenge Success" program notes that 20 to 25 percent of high school students experience depression, and 95 percent admit to cheating.[7] The case against excessive competition in schools was also brought to film in the documentary *Race to Nowhere*. This film poignantly highlights how students are subjected to excessive pressure to succeed, thus falling into a trap of having too much homework, too many tests, and too little free time. The ones that succeed on this path often end up burned out, lacking curiosity, or unable to appreciate the true joy of learning.[8]

So if excessive competition, grades, and test scores aren't the best predictors of success and happiness, then what are? In a fascinating book, *How Children Succeed*, author Paul Tough argues that certain character traits are the true predictors of success.[9] Tough points out that many children who are successful by traditional measures often face difficulties in college. He cites the research of the University of Pennsylvania and Angela Duckworth, who noted that children who have certain traits consistently succeed in college and beyond.

Duckworth's research showed that students with self-control, for example, tended to be more successful and that this was also a more reliable predictor of a student's GPA than an IQ score. However, her research also noted another trait that was a better predictor of high achievers, a trait she refers to as "grit."[10] Grit is defined in two parts: 1) passion for a certain goal and 2) persistence to overcome obstacles that may appear in reaching that goal.

I have a personal story that illustrates this definition of grit. The high school football team I am a member of, the Grapevine Mustangs, experienced several consecutive unsuccessful seasons. Consequently, our team pride was fading, the community was weary of our accumulating losses, students were making fun of us, and the team altogether was falling apart. However, in my junior year, a new coaching staff was recruited. This new group of coaches re-instilled our craving for victory. Our passion for the game and our burning desire to win became stronger than ever.

Our off-season practices became exponentially more difficult, as our workouts mirrored those led by successful college teams. Our methods also incorporated other sports, such as wrestling, to further build our mental and physical toughness. This model became a source of attraction for the local media. Newscasters would stop by to interview Head Coach Randy Jackson and report on our unprecedented off-season methods.[11] Coaches from other high schools and even some colleges were impressed with our new techniques. This illustrates how grit, which our team kept alive despite failure and adversity, was an essential characteristic for achievement and success.

In addition to grit, Duckworth also cites social intelligence, gratitude, optimism, and curiosity as character traits essential for predicting success.[12] Moreover, maintaining the proper balance of these traits is just as important. Such character traits can't be taught like an academic subject, but are often formed through trial and error and by taking risks without anyone else to coddle us through. "The idea of building grit and building self-control is that you get that through failure," explains Dominic Randolph, headmaster of Riverdale Country School, a private school in New York. "Yet, ironically, in most highly academic environments in the United States, no one fails anything."[12]

I believe there is one other factor that contributes to sound character development and success in school: physical activity. For years, the emphasis on physical activity in the educational system has been waning, and, in fact, it is no longer required in many secondary schools. The current institutional attitude toward physical activity is one of little weight. The theory is that school time should focus on academic subjects. Yet current research is better establishing the link between increasing physical activity and improved learning and grades. A recent study by the American College of Sports Medicine discovered that college students who regularly exercise get better grades. This conclusion is notable because it is the first time that this kind of link has been shown in college students.[13] Along the same lines, another study showed a positive correlation between the number of hours that a student studied and the number of hours that the same student exercised: "Compared with students who studied less than an hour per day, students who studied three or more hours a day were nearly four times more likely to participate in vigorous exercise."[14]

These references are interesting because one could argue that the amount of homework is not the issue. The issue is the student's attitude toward the homework. Based on the research above, this is true, and it is also true that the attitude toward homework improves with exercise. On the other hand, the attitude and objectives of the teacher with respect to the basis for assigning homework are also of importance. Addressing both sides of the coin will ensure a much-improved culture toward learning. For instance, during my freshman year of high school, I was taking AP Human Geography, a challenging course at the freshman level. I was struggling throughout the year to maintain an A and would spend hours a night reading boring pages from my boring textbook. But by the second semester, the homework load reduced. The class rigor actually increased, but work to be done outside of school dramatically reduced. Because of this, I stopped spending hours a night reading from a textbook and was able to relax a little more than I was used to. During this time period, my grades actually improved in my class. I did not change my study habits but merely relaxed more than I had previously. In turn, my grades started to consistently become low As. However, during my free time, I was watching TV instead of being active.

After about six weeks, I changed that habit. I began to play basketball after I ate lunch and would spend more time outside after school hours. My homework level still remained the same (my study habits remained consistent as well), but my physical activity had increased. My grades again improved and I found the class more enjoyable. All of this leads to one key point: the theory that greater amounts of homework improve test scores is a mere misconception and not nearly as effective as proper rest and physical activity. Learning for Generation Z is being transformed by rapid changes in society and in technology. The best comment about how attitudes toward learning can take a giant leap forward in this generation has been most eloquently stated by Deborah Stipek, dean of Stanford University's School of Education:

> Extensive research shows that students will become more emotionally engaged (and even passionate) if simple principles are followed: if the subject matter is connected to students' personal lives and interests; if

students have opportunities to be actively involved in solving or designing solutions to novel and multidimensional problems, doing experiments, debating the implications of findings, or working collaboratively; if students have multiple opportunities to earn a good grade (by rewriting papers or retaking tests); if attention is drawn to the knowledge and skills that students are developing, not to grades or scores; and if all learning and skill development is celebrated, whatever the level . . . problem-solving skills and critical analysis have become infinitely more important than being able to answer the typical questions given on standardized tests.[15]

Notes

1. Natalie Wolchover, "Too Much Homework Is Bad for Kids," *LiveScience*, March 30, 2012, http://www.livescience.com/19379 -homework-bad-kids.html.

2. Mollie Galloway and Denise Pope, "Hazardous Homework? The Relationship Between Homework, Goal Orientation, and Well -Being in Adolescents," *ENCOUNTER* 20, no. 4 (2007): 25–31.

3. John W. Gardner Center, *Youth in the Middle*, 2010, http:// gardnercenter.stanford.edu/docs/YIM_Toolkit_100429.pdf.

4. "Youth in the Middle (YiM) Work Area 3," John W. Gardner Center, 2014, http://gardnercenter.stanford.edu/our_work/YiM _Guide_Work-Area-3.html.

5. Challenge Success, *The Advanced Placement Program: Living Up To Its Promise?*, 2013, http://www.challengesuccess.org/portals/0 /docs/challengesuccess-advancedplacement-wp.pdf.

6. Alfie Kohn, "The Case Against Competition," *Working Mother*, September 1987, http://www.alfiekohn.org/parenting/tcac .htm.

7. "Why It's Important," Challenge Success, 2012, http://www .challengesuccess.org/WhyItsImportant.aspx.

8. Vicki Abeles, *Race to Nowhere* (Reel Link Films, 2010), DCP, 85 min, http://www.racetonowhere.com.

9. Paul Tough, *How Children Succeed: Grit, Curiosity, and the Hidden Power of Character* (New York: Mariner Books, 2013).

10. Angela Lee Duckworth, "The Key to Success? Grit," TED video, 6:12, filmed April 2013, http://www.ted.com/talks/angela_lee _duckworth_the_key_to_success_grit.

11. Ryan Osborne, "Winter Months Are 'Where Your Football Team Is Built,'" *DFW Varsity*, February 11, 2015, http://www.dfw .com/2015/02/11/968350/winter-months-are-where-your -football.html

12. Paul Tough, "What if the Secret to Success Is Failure?" *New York Times Magazine*, September 14, 2011, http://www.nytimes.com/2011/09/18/magazine/what-if-the-secret-to-success-is-failure.html.

13. American College of Sports Medicine, "Hit the Treadmill – Not Just the Books – To Boost Grades," news release, August 1, 2011, http://www.acsm.org/about-acsm/media-room/acsm-in-the-news/2011/08/01/hit-the-treadmill---not-just-the-books---to-boost-grades.

14. Tara Parker-Pope, "Vigorous Exercise Linked With Better Grades," *Well* (blog), *New York Times,* June 3, 2010, http://well.blogs.nytimes.com/2010/06/03/vigorous-exercise-linked-with-better-grades.

15. Deborah Stipek, "Education Is Not a Race," *Science* 332, no. 6037 (June 24, 2011): 1481, doi:10.1126/science.1209339.

Chapter 7

Voting and Political Beliefs:
Why We Think What We Think

The topic of politics has always been of great interest to me and to my family, so it was natural for me to talk about the 2012 election between Barack Obama and Mitt Romney with family and friends. At one point during the campaign that year, I was eating lunch at school with a group of about ten friends. Like any typical teenager, I had friends who ranged from athletic to academic, from pranksters to conservatives, and from timid to outspoken. I didn't realize it then, but I had quite the representation of personalities at my table when I casually brought up the presidential election and asked for whom each person would vote and why. I did not expect that every person had made up their mind and favored a candidate, but they had. However, I soon discovered that none of them had arrived at a conclusion through their own individual research.

I decided to play devil's advocate and purposefully disagree with almost every comment that came out of my friends' mouths. My goal was to prompt them to realize that they had no idea what they were talking about. I knew that political discussions can elicit a range of emotions, but even I was surprised by the scene that took place next. In fact, one friend threw his hands in the air while rolling his eyes and yelled, "The new things Obama wants to implement are gonna do nothing but screw us."

I was amused by the unnecessary, grandiose arm flailing and the intensity of his comment. I chuckled and replied—a bit sarcastically—by saying, "Can you tell me what you mean? I don't understand your quite dramatic remark." He looked at me and said, "If you want to understand what I'm saying, ask my dad." I asked why he could not tell me himself what he meant. He acknowledged that he did not really know the facts but added, "That's beside the point. Obama is gonna screw us all!" At this point, I was laughing fairly hard at his comments, which I viewed as farcical given their lack of grounding. I told him I did not see how he could make these accusations and expect anyone to take them seriously if he did not know what he was saying. He understood my point and admitted that he actually did not know anything at all.

After his confession, many other friends confessed they were simply siding with their parents and had not watched the candidates' debates, heard their speeches, or closely followed the election as a whole. The conversation that ensued was enlightening; we all started Googling the debate questions and watching YouTube video clips of the nominees' responses. We chuckled, paused videos, and voiced opinions on everything from their expressions to their answers. The bell soon rang, and we all dispersed to our classes, but I knew we would soon pick up where we left off.

Previously, I had understood that many kids are greatly influenced by their parents' way of being, but I had not realized to what degree. In a few short years, these young adults would be eligible to vote, and they already had extreme points of view from parental influence. Now comes the big question: When do kids break away from strong parental influence? According to James Marcia, a developmental psychologist, teens begin to make independent political decisions once they reach their college years.[1] But despite evidence showing that young adults are less reliant on their parents' opinions as they make decisions later in life, past influences do not entirely wane. If a strong Republican community surrounds a child, she will most likely vote for a Republican candidate when she can legally vote (the same is true if the child grows up surrounded by Democrats— she is more likely to vote for Democratic candidates). The environment influences a teen's future voting patterns from early childhood.[2] In the future, adults tend to lean toward the political party they were taught was "superior."

What surprised me was the fact that future political decisions of these young people were being shaped right now subconsciously. But why do our parents have such a strong influence on our political attitudes? I believe it is because teens view their parents as experienced or knowledgeable (whether they want to admit it or not). Therefore, we trust our parents' opinions when an issue may appear disputable. There are many layers to grasp in order to understand a party's fundamental goals or a presidential candidate's ideologies. If one wants to truly understand the underpinnings of the political world, then one needs to undertake research, reading, and networking. These are skills that many teens and young adults are not willing to master. But when a child sees their parents watching the election proceedings, they assume that the parents are doing the work to understand what each candidate believes.

So why should we watch the election and "waste" our time on an activity that many of us find boring when we can rely on our parents to do it instead? We already agree with our parents on many issues (except, of course, when it involves restrictions placed on us like our curfew or money-spending habits), so what makes politics different? The problem with this rationale is that it means we fail to realize that our parents could be watching the elections from a possibly biased viewpoint. Our parents likely also grew up siding with the same party or type of candidate; their attitudes were shaped long ago in their youth just as ours are being shaped today. The probability of our parents having suddenly changed their perspective is quite slim. Therefore, we should attempt to keep our minds unpolluted by thoughts that favor one party over another. We should start fresh and do the work to find out whom to support based on our personal beliefs, not on our parent's beliefs. Instead of identifying ourselves with our parents, we should strive to create our own political identity. After all, isn't that what we complain about all the time? We do not want to be seen as the same as our parents—we are going to be much cooler than they are!

It appears that regardless of our gender, race, political background, or generation, we are taking our right to vote for granted, and this prevents us from initiating the work required to become informed voters. Our right to vote is a special one. As of the 1990s, only about half of the world's countries have given their citizens the right to vote, according to Randolf J. Rummel, Professor Emeritus of Political Science at the University of Hawaii.[3] There are many dictatorships around the world, and thus millions of people who are not given this prestigious privilege. In countries such as North Korea, its citizens do not have the right to choose representatives; there, the "Democratic Front for the Reunification of the Fatherland" selects candidates. North Koreans are then required to vote for or against one of these preselected candidates, which in reality is merely a confirmatory vote.[4] Obviously, this is not a true exercise of the freedom to vote.

In contrast, the United States grants its citizens the free and fair right to vote, as any eligible citizen can be a potential candidate for office. However, did you know that for the 2012 elections, only 58 percent of the eligible voters turned out to vote? Did the other 42 percent believe that their vote would not have made a difference? Were they busy or unaware of the elections? As another election approaches, ask yourself and others around you these questions to determine their answers. In 2012, I asked around, and these were some of the reasons many voting adults offered me for not voting:

1. "I live in a state that is predominately Republican. My vote for the Democratic party candidate won't make a difference."

   Although this may be true with respect to winning the electoral votes at a state level, is it not important for us to know as a nation where all the individuals stand?

   Moreover, views can change over time, and these changes can only be appreciated by all of us if all votes are counted, even if there is no immediate impact on the current election.

2. "My wife and I vote for opposite parties, so we'll cancel each other out."

   While this appears logical at first, the logic is overly simplistic. While the media often focuses on one particular race, in most elections, there are numerous positions that must be voted upon. In some races, there are independent candidates or candidates outside of the traditional two-party system. So it behooves us to vote, regardless of what vote we anticipate may be made by someone in the same household or by anyone else in the community.

3. "I didn't like any of the candidates."

Again, the logic seems simple and compelling. This group believes they need to vote for their favorite candidate, one that they highly preferred over another. After all, why vote for a candidate if you think he or she does not deserve the position to be filled? But life is not always that clearly defined. If the position is going to be filled, should you not weigh in since one of those candidates will soon represent you? Should you not at least pick the candidate you dislike the least?

4. "I was too busy."

Really? As I talked to this group, I soon concluded that "I was too busy" was an easy, go-to excuse because the person did not see the full importance, impact, or power of their vote. Many citizens do not realize that one can vote by mail with an absentee ballot or vote early when lines are generally short. Voting is easier than one might think, and often the impact is extraordinary.

For instance, two decades ago South Africa underwent an extraordinary round of elections. The country once operated under a system of racial segregation known as apartheid. The majority of South African citizens were (and still are) black, but were not allowed to vote. Apartheid created horrible conditions for black South Africans, who were relegated to separate bathrooms (which were almost always less sanitary), forced to drink from separate water fountains, and were required to attend separate restaurants and schools. This led to an inferior education for them and an inferior life overall. Any black South African who protested publically against apartheid was often physically assaulted, tortured, or occasionally executed.[5]

With the end of apartheid in 1994, black citizens finally had the right to vote.

These South Africans, having a particular freedom for the first time, did not take it for granted. Many took this election seriously. Families even discussed the elections with their children, and the campaign of every presidential candidate was carefully scrutinized. A large number of South Africans participated in the voting, and Nelson Mandela was elected president.

As president, Nelson Mandela accomplished many goals and contributed to world peace, for which he was awarded the Nobel Peace Prize in 1993. Mandela worked hard to create a unified country and is remembered as one of the greatest figures of our time. Great leaders can be elected when citizens take their elections seriously and vote for the candidate they truly believe will make a difference.

Each individual vote can have a significant impact on our country. However, we must keep in mind that it is our attitude toward voting which is most essential. There is no point in casting a vote unless we know *why* we are voting. We need to be passionate and cognizant of our rationale. If we all remember that we have the possibility of changing things for the better, one vote at a time, then perhaps everyone's attitude toward voting will turn from "not necessary" to "frankly imperative." As Gen Zers reach adulthood, it remains to be seen if we will counter the tide toward voter apathy. One cause for hope is our genuine interest in global issues and social justice.

Notes

1. Mary Madormo, "Parents Influence Children's Political Attitudes," First Vote 2012 (blog), November 30, 2011, http://firstvote2012 .wordpress.com/2011/11/30/parents-influence-childrens -political-attitudes.

2. Kayla Bunge, "Party-Training: Parents' Influence on Children's Political Attitudes Is Powerful," GazetteXtra, October 24, 2008, http:// www.gazettextra.com/news/2008/oct/24/party-training -parents-influence-childrens-politic.

3. "Democratic Peace Clock," Randolph J. Rummel, accessed November 1, 2014, http://www.hawaii.edu/powerkills/dp.clock.htm.

4. "North Korea," *Freedom Barometer*, http://freedombarometer.org /asia.45.html?country_id=23&year=2013.

5. "Quick Facts: Apartheid," StandWithUs, 2014, http://www.askisrael .org/facts/qpt.asp?fid=9.

We can complain because rose bushes have thorns, or rejoice because thorn bushes have roses.

—*Unknown*

Part 3

Perspectives

Take a look at the above picture. Some see a candlestick first, while others see two faces. Perspective makes all the difference. But how do our perspectives affect our decision making or our approach to life? Are we aware that things are not always what they first seem?

When there is a traffic accident, police ask for witnesses to come forward to describe what happened. Yet when witnesses are removed from the incident, they often have varying perspectives on what happened, depending on whether they were the driver or a pedestrian, or whether they were near to or far from the action, or whether they felt they were in danger or were observing from a safe distance. The same principle applies to everything—each situation, event, or conversation has a different meaning to all those involved. We attribute different meanings to events based on how we are affected. In other words, we all have our own realities. One author, Anaïs Nin, states it more eloquently: "We do not see things as they are, we see them as we are."[1] The meanings or perspectives we possess develop when we blend our identity with our attitudes to create a unique way of approaching a situation. These perspectives help us make sense of situations—and of our lives.

But do we always appreciate that our perspective on a situation may be one of many? Or are we likely to believe that we are right and others are wrong? And how willing are we to change our perspective? Are we still open to new facts after we develop a perspective? How can we develop the ability to examine and explore other perspectives besides the ones we are predisposed toward? How can doing so enrich our experience of others, of the world, and of our own lives? These questions matter because they help us understand how we formulate and adjust our perspective, especially in a rapidly changing world where information is updated every second and perspectives can go "viral" within minutes.

Studies of how we develop perspectives often reveal surprising results. According to a popular TV program, *Brain Games*, our brains provide us with the least amount of information necessary in order to make sense of the world.[2] In other words, we are constantly glossing over information (including information that we think we processed fully) in order to keep moving with our day. Many times we fool ourselves into pretending we know something rather than admit that we do not. This is one approach to exerting control over ourselves and of making definitive decisions rather than getting bogged down by a myriad of choices that we have to make every day. The power of positive thinking and of suggestive thinking (the "placebo" effect) also play a significant role in how perspectives develop.

In order to appreciate other perspectives, we must first be able to recognize our own shortcomings. Only then can we truly take steps forward and learn a new method of doing, being, or reasoning that we may not have considered before. We need to be humble and open to the concept that there are perspectives out there that we do not even know we do not know.

Changing cultural values have shaped Gen Z perspectives. An obvious example of this is the loss of clearly defined gender and parent roles. Our generation expects to encounter male nurses as often as they do female doctors. In my home, I grew up thinking that dads do the laundry because I grew up in a household with two working parents where chores were split up according to "who was good at it" rather than "who should do it." When I was in middle school, I was the one who was embarrassed to go to the gym with my little sister because I knew she was a gymnast and had better upper body strength than I did at that time.

A recent survey supports these changing perspectives. The Intelligence Group recently surveyed nine hundred fourteen- to thirty-four-year-olds and concluded that gender identity now is seen as more flexible, without clearly defined norms, and subject to more of a personal interpretation. While there are still roadblocks to gender equality, at least there is widespread acceptance in my generation that males and females can do virtually anything that the other can do.

In the following chapters, I will explore perspectives on topics important to Generation Z, examine the extent to which we are aware of the background from which our perspectives grow, and discuss how flexible our perspectives are when adopting and adapting to new information. I will explore the multifarious perspectives that can arise from a single word or definition. I will discuss hidden perspectives on race, science, and gender. I will revisit the role of social media in the context of Gen Z's perspective on technology and the digital sphere, and I will review where Gen Z's perspectives on civil liberties and politics may be headed.

Notes

1. Anaïs Nin, *The Quotable Anaïs Nin* (San Antonio, TX: Sky Blue Press, 2010).

2. "What You Don't Know," *Brain Games*, season 2, episode 6, aired May 13, 2013.

Chapter 8

Fluid Definitions in Science and Society

In part 2, I talked about an experience I had at a summer camp I attended called Duke TIP. At this camp, I took a three-week course on neuroscience and became intrigued with the anatomy of the brain. In this class, along with talking about how our minds work, we also learned about different mental illnesses and researched case studies pertaining to these diseases. The disorder we discussed the most was autism, and a man named Derek Paravicini was among our case studies.

After every unit in our class, we would divide into groups and give a presentation about the topic we had studied. After our autism unit, a group comprised of three students stood up in front of the class and summarized what we had learned. Autistic individuals, although technically considered to have a neurodevelopmental disorder, sometimes obtain extreme, superhuman powers. This occurs because autism can lead to one area of the brain dominating over other areas. This, in turn, decreases the ability of some neural pathways, but can vastly strengthen others. An excellent illustration of this is the man I mentioned earlier, Derek Paravicini, upon whom our class's presenters on autism focused.

Derek has become well known for his extraordinary power. He was featured on the TV series *Stan Lee's Superhumans,* where he received the title "Super Human."[1] Because Derek is both autistic and blind, the region of his brain that processes music has replaced the region of his brain involving communication and sight. Derek was born blind and cannot even hold up three fingers when asked, but he displays a unique intelligence when seated in front of a piano. When requested, Derek will play any song that he has ever heard, no matter how long it has been since he heard the song. Derek can still play songs with extreme accuracy even if he has not listened to or played the song in fifty years. He can also play a particular piece of music and adapt it to a particular composer's style. Derek can even play back a song with near perfection when he's only just heard it for the first time. These astonishing abilities are what many would consider impossible for a human being to achieve.

At the end of their presentation, the students asked the class a question: Should our definition of intelligence change so that persons with autism who display an extraordinary ability would be considered smart rather than considered mentally disabled? Initially I thought the answer would simply be "they are smart." But the more I thought about it, the more I realized the complexity of the question. In my response to the class, I said that we should *not* change our current definition of intelligence because although we may be encompassing those that are brilliant but autistic, we would also be excluding others who are brilliant but labeled as "disabled" due to the context in which we interact with them. If we were to alter the definition of intelligence to add "and autistic persons who possess an extraordinary ability like no other," we would then be excluding all the other developmentally disabled who may possess a special ability of which we are unaware or don't quite perceive as "extraordinary" or "superhuman."

Although society may need to determine a definition of "intelligence" or of other words that describe mental capabilities for medical, legal, or research purposes, we must also be able to define such words in a manner that acknowledges several different perspectives. Gen Z does not approach the traditional definitions of roles—or even identities—as set in stone in the way that previous generations have. This is supported by a recent survey of nine hundred teens and young adults conducted by the JWT Intelligence Group. Their survey noted that only 25 percent of men feel that portrayals of their gender in ads are accurate. In the same survey, four in ten women preferred clothing or products made specifically for men. And more than two-thirds of those surveyed agreed that gender does not define a person to the extent that it once did.[2]

I believe the same view needs to be taken with those whom we categorize as "mentally retarded" or as having a "developmental disability." We need to realize that such definitions are not set in stone but can be fluid, changing with the pace of scientific discovery, cultural values, and technology. The new perspectives we form should push to change outdated definitions that imply inaccurate and unproductive meanings.

In high school, there are various types of cliques, but typically, kids tend to group themselves along a dichotomy—such as the spirited athletes versus the studious academics. The academics see themselves as cool because they are witty, smart, and preparing for a successful future. The athletes think they are cool because they know how to have fun and enjoy challenging themselves physically. Both of these groups consider

themselves "cool," but how could this one word with one definition apply to two groups on completely opposite ends of the
spectrum?

One definition has many interpretations. One word can be
looked at in various ways. Our perspective is always key.

People who have autism may actually look at others like
my classmates and me and think we are the ones lacking vital
abilities. In my opinion, they have every right to do so. Someone like Derek may believe that the rest of the population lacks
what he considers a "normal" ability; he could think we are the
ones who are developmentally disabled. According to his possible interpretation of smart and intelligent, he would be the
brilliant one. However, in our interpretation of the same words,
we imply that Derek is developmentally disabled and position
ourselves as the intelligent ones. We agree on the definitions but
disagree on the interpretations.

If we change the definition of a word such as "intelligence,"
we would only add to the confusion. Instead, we need to grasp
that a definition and our interpretation of it fall hand in hand
and can coexist. A definition shifts based on a person's interpretation; one influences the other. Thus, it does no good to
change one or the other. Instead, it is essential to understand
how one affects the other in order for us to realize how different
perspectives come about.

So, definitions may be fluid and subject to change, but is it
possible to test the validity of a perspective?

One of my favorite classes in school was the lab portion of
my science classes. I found it thrilling to get out of the seat and
use my hands and brain together in order to answer a scientific question and discover the results firsthand. I found science,
like math, logical and straightforward, even when I did not understand all the concepts immediately. It was still possible to

make a hypothesis, test it, and interpret results relative to the hypothesis. Then, others in the class could validate or invalidate our findings. In either case, over time we drew conclusions that were easier to remember because we had discovered the answers for ourselves.

Through this approach, we become participants in science, a field that requires critical thinking, acquiring skills, sharing results, undergoing peer review, and having others verify the results. Through this same process, we have advanced society. Yet when I turn on the TV, read the newspaper, or access the Internet, I encounter attacks on and attempts to invalidate science. It seems that many do not trust science because they do not understand it or because they feel that some expert wants to tell them what to believe. On a deeper level, some feel that they cannot be expected to follow the guidelines that arise out of scientific conclusions they do not understand—that this would be a violation of their democratic principles.

Still others see science as something that is heard on the local news, which then needs to be valued and judged according to a personal belief system. People are more likely to learn about climate change from their favorite TV reporter or talk show host than they are from a scientific expert with a background in climatology. In this context, many see the scientific information presented as a threat to their religious or political beliefs. In fact, "Politically, we may be moving more and more toward a world where our beliefs are shaped not by what is actually true, but instead by the pseudo-realities created by talk shows and political pundits," says Dietram Scheufele, professor of Life Sciences Communication at UW-Madison.[3]

There is a difference between what science tells us about the world and how we choose to or are able to process and apply this information. Science may be able to describe for us what can be discovered, created, or achieved, but science cannot tell us if we ought to take these steps and what benefit or detriment may result. Our inability to distinguish between these two concepts puts some people at odds with the science itself, and they consider it a threat.

More interesting is a body of research called *motivated reasoning*. In this concept drawn from the field of psychology, researchers explore how our personal beliefs and attitudes influence and often limit our ability to accept scientific facts as real. The good news is that our limitations that lead to motivational reasoning can be overcome by better communication from scientists regarding how they arrived at their findings. It is important to realize that insights into how the public receives and interprets research may be just as important as the original scientific research itself. The significance of this issue has caught the attention of the National Academy of Sciences, which held a recent conference in Washington, DC, fully devoted to the topic of "The Science of Science Communication."[4]

New research from Duke University provides another twist to our understanding of how perspectives on science develop. This research, by Troy Campbell and Aaron Kay and published in the *Journal of Personality and Social Psychology*, shows that our personal beliefs can actually prevent us from accepting solutions to issues because we instead deny that the problem even exists.[5] In the study, two hundred participants were asked if they agreed with the assessment that climate change caused by human activities would raise the Earth's temperature by 3.2 degrees Fahrenheit during this century. When the participants thought that a solution to prevent climate change would be only a minor inconvenience, they were more likely to agree that the Earth's temperature would rise. However, when the participants thought that a solution could potentially lead to a more significant impact on their lifestyle or the economy, they were more likely to disagree that Earth's temperature would rise. The more action these individuals thought they had to undertake themselves, the less likely they were to agree that action on their part was necessary or that the threat was even real. If they had to buy an environmentally friendly car and a "green" house to prevent climate change, then they became more likely to deny the existence of climate change altogether.

However, in one subgroup, the participants were informed that there existed a free-market solution involving green technologies that would also boost the economy. The percentage of this group that agreed with the global warming assessment jumped from 22 percent to 55 percent.

In the next experiment, Campbell and Kay focused on test participants who favored strict gun control laws. These participants were given a passage to read that stated that homeowners who had access to guns actually experienced a fewer number of violent home invasions. This passage contradicted the belief of the participants who held that more restrictions on guns were better. The passage instead implied that the more guns that were issued to American citizens, the less violence there would be; more guns would create a safer environment. After reading a passage that presented a solution contrary to their beliefs, the test participants were less likely to acknowledge gun violence as an issue of great importance, a view that indicated a complete change in opinion from what they had believed before reading the passage.

These studies point toward a specific phenomenon within the realm of motivated reasoning called *solution aversion*. In other words, "if you feel really negatively about the solution, if you don't want the solution to happen, then you deny that the problem exists," according to Campbell.[6] It is important for us to look at these studies in such a way that they can help us see "the tendency of people to change their factual beliefs to fit their moral inclinations," as succinctly stated by Peter Ditto, an expert on motivated reasoning at UC-Irvine.[6]

Let's look at another controversial science topic with opposing perspectives: vaccines. Andrew Wakefield published the initial study that provided a link between vaccines and autism in 1998. Wakefield was subsequently censored in the United Kingdom by the General Medical Council, which ruled that he acted dishonestly and without approval from an ethics committee. Further investigation showed that a group that had a vested interest in his conclusions paid the author a large sum of money.[7] In the United States, even the CDC noted "an overwhelming body of research by the world's leading scientists that concludes there is no link between MMR vaccine and autism."[8] Yet despite the widespread disrepute of this study, many parents continue to deny their children potentially lifesaving vaccines based on a fear that these vaccines could induce autism.

In a 2002 study, researchers interviewed parents of children who were diagnosed with autism.[9] These parents often reported different onset times of their child's autism in different interviews. This study concluded that "the history given by the parents had changed after the extensive publicity about MMR vaccine and autism. Before the publicity, the parents often reported concerns early in their child's life, usually before their first birthday; the current history for the same children recorded symptoms as developing only after MMR vaccination, in some cases shortly after." Why do such perspectives about scientific topics, where facts can be clearly and definitively presented, persist despite being debunked by experts and scientific agencies? The answer lies in a common and growing tactic in the media whereby opposite perspectives are often portrayed as two equally relevant views. With this approach, scientific certainty becomes just another issue for two people to "debate" on television.

Fortunately, studies have shown that subtle changes in how science news is presented can make a big difference in how that news is perceived. In one study from the University of Wisconsin-Madison, participants were given one of three descriptions of nanotechnology.[10] One definition described nanotechnology's unique applications, another focused on its risks and benefits, and a third explained the unique applications as well as the risks and benefits. The researchers then evaluated the participants' level of support for nanotechnology and their interest in learning more. They found that if the description solely highlighted nanotechnology's useful applications, the participants were more likely to support nanotechnology, but not more likely to obtain additional information. If the description focused on risks and benefits, participants were interested in learning more, but less likely to support nanotechnology. This, of course, has significant implications for researchers who wish to engage the public in areas of science that are not yet fully accepted or understood.

The role of search engines is another major factor in the development of perspectives and opinions. When people choose one of Google's top suggested articles or links, they click on one of the high-rated results for that search. But Google bases its suggestions on the number of clicks a result receives. As Dominique Brosssard, a professor at the University of Wisconsin-Madison, notes, "Sergey Brin and Larry Page created Google to sort search results, in part, based on how popular particular sites were. For science information, that means that surfers may be offered the most popular results rather than the ones that best represent the current state of the science."[11]

Even if you find a well-written and well-researched scientific piece on the Internet, your perspective of the facts presented may be influenced by another factor unbeknownst to you: the comments section at the bottom. In fact, *Popular Science* magazine recently shut off the comments on their website for precisely this reason. In a scathing editorial, Suzanne LaBarre, the online content director, says that "even a fractious minority wields enough power to skew a reader's perception of a story."[12] LaBarre goes on to reference another interesting study by Brossard, in which 1,183 Americans read a fake blog post on nanotechnology and were then surveyed on how they felt about the topic. The study conditions exposed half the group to civil comments and the other half to rude or insulting comments that included phrases such as "you're an idiot" or "you're stupid if you're not thinking of the risks." Brossard called the results "both surprising and disturbing" because the uncivil comments often changed the reader's view of the news story itself. In other words, "simply including an ad hominem attack in a reader comment was enough to make study participants think the downside of the reported technology was greater than they'd previously thought."[13]

Gen Z, growing up in an era when we can see how easy it is to define, label, and redefine somebody, is sensitive to how information is portrayed. We understand that scientific information is often presented out of context, and at the same time, we recognize how impressionable and influenced we are. We understand that our perspectives, whether on the definition of a word or on topics like scientific studies, are largely affected by our attitudes. These attitudes can be influenced positively or negatively depending on how that information is presented. We are aware nonetheless that our perspectives will then impact the public debate in much the same way that clicks on a Google search impact what results you might find. We must hold ourselves responsible, both in the content of our discussions as well as in the tone, as both can substantially influence the debate in the online era.

Notes

1. "Human Speed Bump," *Stan Lee's Superhumans,* season 1, episode 4, aired August 26, 2010.

2. The Intelligence Group, *The Cassandra Gender Report,* 2013, http://www.cassandra.co/wp-content/themes/trendcentral /pdfs/Gender%20Report%20-%20Media%20Memo%20-%20 SUFL2013.pdf.

3. Terry Devitt, "Is Media-Driven 'Pseudo-Reality' the Future of U.S. Politics?," *University of Wisconsin-Madison News,* April 10, 2012, http://www.news.wisc.edu/20543.

4. "Agenda – The Science of Science Communication," National Academy of Sciences, May 21-22, 2012, http://www.nasonline.org/ programs/sackler-colloquia/completed_colloquia/agenda -science-communication.html.

5. Troy Campbell and Aaron Kay, "Solution Aversion: On the Relation Between Ideology and Motivated Disbelief," *Journal of Personality and Social Psychology* 107, no. 5 (2014): 809–24.

6. Brandon Keim, "How People's Political Passions Distort Their Sense of Reality," *Wired,* November 19, 2014, http://www.wired .com/2014/11/solutions-shape-factual-belief.

7. David Gorski, "The General Medical Council to Andrew Wakefield: 'The Panel Is Satisfied That Your Conduct Was Irresponsible and Dishonest,'" *Science-Based Medicine* (blog), February 1, 2010, http://www.sciencebasedmedicine.org/andrew-wakefield-the -panel-is-satisfied-that-your-conduct-was-irresponsible-and-dishonest.

8. Gardiner Harris, "Journal Retracts 1998 Paper Linking Autism to Vaccines," *New York Times,* February 2, 2010, http://www .nytimes.com/2010/02/03/health/research/03lancet.html.

9. N. Andrews, E. Miller, B. Taylor, R. Lingam, A. Simmons, J. Stowe, P. Waight, "Recall Bias, MMR, and Autism," *Archives of Disease in Childhood* 87, no. 6 (December 2002): 493–94, doi:10.1136 /adc.87.6.493.

10. Ashley A. Anderson, Jiyoun Kim, Dietram A. Scheufele, Dominique Brossard, Michael A. Xenos, "What's in a Name? How We Define Nanotech Shapes Public Reactions," *Journal of Nanoparticle Research* 15, no. 2 (February 2013): article 1421, doi:10.1007/s11051-013-1421-z.

11. Chris Barncard, "Web Searches May Sacrifice Accuracy for Popularity," *University of Wisconsin-Madison News,* May 18, 2010, http://www.news.wisc.edu/18103.

12. Suzanne LaBarre, "Why We're Shutting Off Our Comments," *Popular Science,* September 24, 2013, http://www.popsci.com/science/article/2013-09/why-were-shutting-our-comments.

13. Dominique Brossard and Dietram A. Scheufele, "This Story Stinks," Gray Matter, *New York Times,* March 2, 2013, http://www.nytimes.com/2013/03/03/opinion/sunday/this-story-stinks.html.

Chapter 9

Overcoming Discrimination in Issues of Gender and Race

During the summer before my freshman year of high school, my sister and her friend wanted to join the same strength and conditioning program that I had already started with my friends. When she brought this up during a family dinner, I hesitated and expressed the embarrassment I would feel if she were to join the same program I was doing with my friends. My parents pounced on me, saying that I shouldn't be embarrassed by my little sister (who is three years junior to me). My mom went on a diatribe about how important it is for girls to have the same opportunities as boys in order to reach their full potential. Puzzled, I explained that I was embarrassed by my sister only because, as a gymnast, she was in excellent shape and I thought she could make me look bad in the strength and conditioning program. My parents were briefly puzzled before breaking out in laughter.

It was at this point that I realized the perspective I had about my sister was very different from the one my parents held.

My parents wanted to get rid of any bias I might have had about females and sports. But I never had any, and we had to realize that it was they and not I who lived in the era when such a perspective was commonplace and acceptable. On the other hand, I grew up respecting and appreciating girls in my grade who could play basketball better than me even though I once played on the school team. I even played against girls on football teams when I was in middle school. But as I have entered high school and grown older, I can tell that gender discrimination still exists although—like racial discrimination—it can be subtle and thus overlooked if you are not paying attention.

For example, in my required classes throughout high school, we usually had an equal number of boys and girls, except for in elective classes such as computer science, where there were hardly any girls. In registering for my senior-year, upper-level physics classes, I was informed that not enough girls had signed up. I asked some of my female friends about this issue, and they told me they were not as interested in those types of classes. When I researched the issue further, I found that it is common for girls and women to give a similar answer. But why? From my perspective, girls were not only doing just as well as boys in sports but also just as well as, if not better than, boys in our core math and science classes. But the more I read, the more I saw it confirmed that although women are pursuing life sciences in greater numbers, many still shy away from math-intensive fields such as computer science and physics.[1] There is still an apparent gender bias in which both men and women seem to view these particular fields as better suited for males.

Carol Dweck, a professor at Stanford, observed that when learning new information that may be confusing, grade-school girls with high IQs handle the confusion much more poorly than boys with high IQs. For girls, the higher their IQ, the worse they did in learning new material after the period of confusion. For boys, on the other hand, the higher the IQ they had, the better they handled the challenge of any new, confusing material.[2]

The difference in reaction has to do with how students cope with experiences when their ability is called into question. Based on gender, that challenge tends to either stimulate students further or demoralize them. The different levels of interest in math in the two genders may have more to do with how one copes with new, potentially confusing material rather than a gender difference in math ability. This, of course, points to the fact that math may currently be taught in a manner that favors males more than females. However, if we assume the perspective that the differing interest between males and females is related to ability and convey that to students, then this alone can undermine the performance of girls in these classes. In another study, female college students answered more questions correctly on math tests when they were told beforehand "college students are good at math" than when they were told "women are bad at math."[3]

But this bias goes all the way down to the grade school level and crosses borders and societies. In one study of middle and high school students that took place in Israel, students were given exams graded by two different teachers: one who knew their names and one who did not.[4] In math exams, the girls scored higher than the boys if the exams were graded anonymously, but the boys scored higher than the girls when they were graded by teachers who knew their names and consequently their genders. This effect could not be reproduced in other subjects such as English. The researchers concluded that in math and science specifically, the teachers overestimated the boys' abilities and underestimated the girls' abilities—and that this had long-term effects on students' attitudes toward the subjects.

Many of us think of gender issues in terms of broad statements such as "In this era, I believe a woman can do anything that a man can do." But research shows that our attitudes about gender have a far more surreptitious impact than what we may consciously realize. One study from the University of Illinois at Urbana-Champaign and Arizona State University showed that female-named hurricanes kill almost twice as many people as similar male-named hurricanes.[5] These findings seem to indicate that we expect male hurricanes to be more violent and deadly, and, as a result, we take less adequate precautions when the hurricane has a female name. The authors of this study also asked participants to predict the intensity and risk level of a hurricane. With all other variables being equal, a hurricane with a male name such as Alexander was predicted to be a more violent storm than a hurricane with a female name like Alexandra. In fact, the participants were more willing to evacuate from a "Hurricane Victor" than a "Hurricane Victoria." And women were as likely as men to give female-named hurricanes less significance. The point is that there is an unconscious bias even among well-meaning persons who openly advocate principles of equality.

These biases continue with social media and online reviews. Benjamin Schmidt, a history professor at Northeastern University, built an online, interactive chart using data from fourteen million student reviews drawn from www.RateMyProfessors.com.[6] After entering a descriptor such as "genius" or "bossy" or "knowledgeable," one can see the frequency of that feedback categorized by gender and academic subject. There are some clear trends that indicate, for instance, that female teachers are more likely to be called "bossy" whereas a male teacher would be called "assertive." Overall, as the *New York Times* reported, the data "suggests that people tend to think more highly of men than women in professional settings, praise men for the same things they criticize women for, and are more likely to focus on a woman's appearance or personality and on a man's skills and intelligence."[7]

The impact of such perspectives on gender roles can even have a significant impact on how judges in the United States interpret legal cases related to gender. A study by the University of Rochester and Harvard University reviewed 2,500 votes by 224 federal appeals courts and made some startling conclusions. It turns out that judges with daughters are more likely to vote in favor of women's rights than ones with only sons.

The effect was most pronounced among male judges appointed by Republican presidents, as well as among judges having one daughter as opposed to one son.[8]

Along with gender bias, racial bias is an issue that many of us in Gen Z realize has made great progress in the last few generations. However, like gender bias, racial bias has become subtle in its manifestation. A few years ago, on a trip to Washington, DC, I stood on the steps of the Lincoln Memorial looking out across the reflecting pool and beyond the World War II Memorial to gaze at the Washington Memorial. I was standing exactly where Martin Luther King Jr. stood when he addressed over two hundred fifty thousand people on August 28, 1963. With this view before me, mixed with my memories of King's "I Have a Dream" speech, I felt truly blessed to be living in such a great country. At that moment, I could truly appreciate how much injustice and discrimination we have overcome in our country that many parts of the world unfortunately still experience.

But on my way back home, reality set in. Just earlier that year, a seventeen-year-old African American named Trayvon Martin was walking home at night after buying some snacks at a convenience store. George Zimmerman, an older white man who lived in the neighborhood, was driving by and became suspicious of the teenager, who was wearing a hoodie while walking in the rain. Zimmerman called 911 to report his concerns that this pedestrian might be a burglar. Unfortunately, by the time police arrived, Zimmerman had left his car against the 911 operator's advice and shot and killed Martin.

Was Zimmerman's suspicious perspective fueled by Martin's race? Did Martin's manner of dress as well as his race lead the driver to judge him as one of those "punks" who "always get away"? Many of my peers thought so. After a jury trial, Zimmerman was acquitted based on a self-defense argument. But how can a teenager who is no longer alive present his perspective? This fact struck a chord with teens around the country. Many of us felt that had the races of the teenager and the driver been switched, the outcome of that night as well as the jury's verdict might have been different.

Even President Obama discussed the issue in a starkly personal manner.[9] He shared the information that when he was a child, he would hear the locks of cars click as he walked across the street. He recalled getting on an elevator and seeing the woman next to him clutch her purse a little more tightly. He would be followed in department stores while shopping. President Obama's words, as spoken from the perspective of an African American, were significant because they noted what Gen Z teens have also noticed: that racial, religious, and gender discrimination are alive and well. The discrimination may not be the same overt kind that Martin Luther King Jr. faced, but it still exists as a subtle and pervasive problem.

Those who have not experienced the subtlety of this problem tend to discount it as nonexistent. But as President Obama mentioned, it is so subtle that even those in the immediate vicinity of this problem may miss it. Gone are the obvious signs from our history—"No Colored People" allowed—but many of us have developed troubling, biased perspectives, sometimes outside of our conscious awareness. Back in part 2, I discussed how attitudes form and argued that our best approach to appreciating differing perspectives is to become cognizant of how our own perspectives have formed.

Howard J. Ross, author of *Everyday Bias*, notes that babies as young as three months old prefer being around people of their own race.[10] A study of racial discrimination in the NBA found that white NBA referees call more fouls on black players and black NBA referees call more fouls on white players with all other factors being equal.[11] Another famous study on racial discrimination from MIT and the University of Chicago involved sending out five thousand fictitious résumés in response to thirteen hundred help-wanted ads. According to Sendhil Mullainathan, one of the authors, the same résumé was roughly 50 percent more likely to result in a callback for an interview if the résumé contained a stereotypically Anglo name (such as Brendan) than if it contained a stereotypically African-American name (such as Jamal).[12] HR managers who reviewed these published findings were surprised since many of them believed that they valued diversity in their companies. The dichotomy between how HR managers actually make *intuitive* decisions about whom to interview versus how they *consciously* think they make those decisions comes down to their attitudes.

When we make slow, deliberate, conscious decisions, we may be more aware of our attitudes. However, when we make quick, intuitive decisions, we are subject to our inherent attitudes, of which we not likely to be fully aware. Most issues involving differences in racial perspectives currently lie within this struggle. As Eduardo Bonilla-Silva, professor and chair of sociology at Duke University, said, "The main problem nowadays is not the folks with the hoods, but the folks dressed in suits."[13] Bonilla-Silva's comment is not likely to be accepted by all Americans, as only 16 percent of white Americans agree that black Americans face significant discrimination, yet 56 percent of black Americans agree.[14]

I believe Gen Z teens are less likely than previous generations to say there is no racism in America. They are more likely to say that discrimination in many forms still exists and that these forms of discrimination are not always visible or tangible. They are situations that can be seen through subtle cues like a woman clutching her purse or a person crossing the street to walk on the other side when he sees a teenager in a hoodie. Gen Z understands how quickly views can form and change on platforms such as social media. We are more likely to offer nuanced responses, knowing as well that the repercussions of saying the wrong thing in our comments could live in perpetuity. Even FBI Director James Comey recently noted that police officers and other law enforcement personnel should avoid "lazy mental short-cuts" that can lead to any kind of bias in the way they profile and treat racial minorities.[15]

These mental shortcuts genuinely concern the parents of minority children. In a televised interview, Charles Blow, a columnist for the *New York Times*, asked viewers a question that touched the hearts of millions across the country: "Is there a right way to hold your body where you do not draw suspicion, or does black masculinity just become suspicious to some people all the time?"[16]

Mr. Blow was referring to the fact that, according to commentators across the country, when a black man is walking fast or running, he may be perceived to be fleeing from a scene and therefore be labeled as suspicious. On the other hand, if the black man is walking slowly, like Trayvon Martin, it may appear to someone like George Zimmerman that he is targeting a house to rob.

Mr. Blow said that he had this conversation with his own kids: Is there a proper way for a black man to walk? He explained to his children that they must be careful and remain aware of their appearance. After he made these remarks on national television, many other African Americans came forward and confessed they have had the same type of conversations with their children as well. Although we have overcome many racial barriers in the history of the United States, many subtle forms of racism still exist. The challenge we face in eradicating this scourge relies on our understanding of attitudes and their role in the development of discriminatory perspectives. Even overt and institutionalized forms of racism begin with attitudes that may have developed long ago. Gen Z's role will be to move beyond law and order in order to address the issue at its root, in the early stages of attitude development, and before racism becomes an established perspective in a person's thoughts. Clearly, this is a challenging issue. However, with a scientific approach and a global online platform, Gen Z is willing to take this challenge on.

Notes

1. "Statistics," National Girls Collaborative, 2015, http://www .ngcproject.org/statistics.

2. Carol S. Dweck, "Is Math a Gift? Beliefs That Put Females at Risk," in *Why Aren't More Women in Science? Top Researchers Debate the Evidence*, ed. S. J. Ceci and W. Williams (Washington, DC: American Psychological Association), https://web .stanford.edu/dept/psychology/cgi-bin/drupalm/system/files /cdweckmathgift.pdf.

3. Robert J. Rydell, Allen R. McConnell, and Sian L. Beilock, "Multiple Social Identities and Stereotype Threat: Imbalance, Accessibility, and Working Memory," *Journal of Personality and Social Psychology* 96, no. 5 (May 2009):949–66, doi:10.1037 /a0014846.

4. Edith Sand and Victor Lavy, "On The Origins of Gender Human Capital Gaps: Short and Long Term Consequences of Teachers' Stereotypical Biases," *National Bureau of Economic Research Working Paper Series*, January 2015, doi:10.3386/w20909.

5. Kiju Jung, Sharon Shavitt, Madhu Viswanathan, and Joseph M. Hilbe, "Female Hurricanes are Deadlier Than Male Hurricanes," *Proceedings of the National Academy of Sciences USA* 111, no. 24 (June 17, 2014): 8782–87, doi:10.1073 /pnas.1402786111.

6. Benjamin M. Schmidt, "Rate My Professor," *BenSchmidt.org* (blog), February 6, 2015, http://benschmidt.org/2015/02/06/rate -my-professor.

7. Claire Cain Miller, "Is the Professor Bossy or Brilliant? Much Depends on Gender," *New York Times*, February 6, 2015, http://www .nytimes.com/2015/02/07/upshot/is-the-professor-bossy-or -brilliant-much-depends-on-gender.html.

8. Adam N. Glynn and Maya Sen, "Identifying Judicial Empathy: Does Having Daughters Cause Judges to Rule for Women's Issues?,"

American Journal of Political Science 59, no. 1 (January 2015): 37–54, doi:10.1111/ajps.12118

9. Washington Post Staff, "President Obama's Remarks on Trayvon Martin (Full Transcript)," *Washington Post,* July 19, 2013, http://www .washingtonpost.com/politics/president-obamas-remarks-on -trayvon-martin-full-transcript/2013/07/19/5e33ebea-f09a -11e2-a1f9-ea873b7e0424_story.html.

10. Howard J. Ross, *Everyday Bias* (Lanham: Rowman & Littlefield, 2014).

11. Joseph Price and Justin Wolfers, "Racial Discrimination Among NBA Referees," *Quarterly Journal of Economics* 125, no. 4 (November 2010): 1859–87, doi:10.1162/qjec.2010.125.4.1859.

12. Sendhil Mullainathan, "Racial Bias, Even When We Have Good Intentions," Economic View, *New York Times,* January 3, 2015, http://www.nytimes.com/2015/01/04/upshot/the -measuring-sticks-of-racial-bias-.html.

13. John Blake, "The New Threat: 'Racism Without Racists,'" CNN, November 27, 2014, http://www.cnn.com/2014/11/26 /us/ferguson-racism-or-racial-bias.

14. Michael A. Fletcher, "Whites Think Discrimination against Whites Is a Bigger Problem Than Bias against Blacks," *Wonkblog, Washington Post,* October 8, 2014, http://www.washingtonpost.com /blogs/wonkblog/wp/2014/10/08/white-people-think -racial-discrimination-in-america-is-basically-over.

15. James B. Comey, "Hard Truths: Law Enforcement and Race," speech, Georgetown University, Washington, DC, February 12, 2015, http://www.fbi.gov/news/speeches/hard-truths-law -enforcement-and-race.

16. Charles M. Blow, "The Whole System Failed Trayvon Martin," The Opinion Pages, *New York Times,* July 15, 2013, http://www .nytimes.com/2013/07/16/opinion/the-whole-system-failed .html.

Chapter 10

Social Media, Civil Liberties, and Politics

Recently, a fourteen-year-old Dutch girl named Sarah tweeted a "joke" at the official American Airlines Twitter account: "@AmericanAir hello my name's Ibrahim and I'm from Afghanistan. I'm part of Al Qaida and on June 1st I'm gonna do something really big bye." She quickly received the response from American Airlines that one would expect, especially in the post-9/11 world: "Sarah, we take these threats very seriously. Your IP address and details will be forwarded to security and the FBI." Sarah quickly recanted with tweets such as "I was kidding pls don't I'm just a girl pls." Her subsequent meltdown on Twitter became an Internet sensation, and she gained thirty thousand followers overnight. She turned herself in and was briefly arrested before being freed.[1]

What I find interesting about this case is the number of young Twitter users who defended Sarah, taking up her cause with other inappropriate tweets such as "@SouthwestAir I bake really good pies and my friends call me 'the bomb' am I still allowed to fly?"[2] Yes, we could call all of these Twitter users idiotic, juvenile, and out of touch with the consequences of their actions. Or we could explore to see if there is a deeper issue present. Are members of Gen Z disconnected by time from the most infamous terrorist attack in modern history, which allows them to tweet something so inappropriate? Or is there a divide among generations in how social media is perceived, especially with regard to privacy and law enforcement?

For example, in order for a comment, which is protected by the First Amendment, to be perceived as a threat, a reasonable observer would have to perceive the missive to communicate a genuine threat.[3] Of course, this broad definition can become complicated when people from different generations are using social media. Police officers, prosecutors, and judges may not be as familiar with the context and cultural cues of Twitter exchanges. What these law enforcement members may see as "trash talk" between two individuals who are communicating over the phone or in a face-to-face conversation may be perceived by them to be a threat if tweeted.

Take, for instance, Justine Sacco, who at the time of this incident was a thirty-year-old senior director of corporate communications at her company. She went from New York to South Africa via London to visit her family. Along her journey, she tweeted about some of the quirks associated with air travel, in some cases being quite sarcastic. One tweet said, "'Weird German Dude: You're in First Class. It's 2014. Get some deodorant.'— Inner monologue as I inhale BO. Thank God for pharmaceuticals."

But it was her last tweet prior to her boarding the long flight to South Africa that changed her life: "Going to Africa. Hope I don't get AIDS. Just kidding. I'm white!" By the time she landed in London, her tweet had been retweeted by Sam Biddle, an editor of a tech-industry blog, to his fifteen thousand followers.

This led to thousands of vitriolic comments about what an awful, privileged person Sacco must believe she is. As part of the aftermath from this comment, she eventually lost her job.

But upon further reflection, this is what Jon Ronson wrote in the *New York Times* about her situation: "I could understand why some people found it offensive. Read literally, she said that white people don't get AIDS, but it seems doubtful many interpreted it that way. More likely it was her apparently gleeful flaunting of her privilege that angered people. But after thinking about her tweet for a few seconds more, I began to suspect that it wasn't racist but a reflexive critique of white privilege—on our tendency to naïvely imagine ourselves immune from life's horrors. Sacco, like Stone, had been yanked violently out of the context of her small social circle. Right?"[4]

Ronson later met up with Sacco to ask her for her own take on the situation. During the course of this conversation, she said, "To me it was so insane of a comment for anyone to make. I thought there was no way that anyone could possibly think it was literal." One year later, Biddle, the blogger who brought her tweet to viral status, had dinner with Sacco, calling her "friendly, very funny, instantly relatable, and very plainly not a cruel sicko. We talked about college, jobs, home, family, and work." In his one-year anniversary blog, Biddle issued a public apology for ruining her life.[5]

As Ronson so eloquently summed up in his analysis of this situation: "Social media is so perfectly designed to manipulate our desire for approval, and that is what led to her undoing. Her tormentors were instantly congratulated as they took Sacco down bit by bit, and so they continued to do so. Their motivation was much the same as Sacco's own—a bid for the attention of strangers—as she milled about Heathrow, hoping to amuse people she couldn't see."[4] The bottom line is that many persons, especially those younger than Justine Sacco, feel that the online world is merely an extension of the real world and should therefore be subject to the same kind of nuanced controls and contexts.

In other words, we should be able to distinguish real threats while allowing for the same kind of commentary, sarcasm, banter, and other idioms that form the basis of communication in the real world.

In understanding the forces that shape our perspective on civil liberties such as freedom of speech, it is important to understand what types of events and what periods of our lives most influence our outlook on the government's role. According to Karl Mannheim, one of the founders of classical sociology in the early twentieth century, people are disproportionately influenced by events that occur between their late teens and early twenties.[6, 7] It is during this time of life that we are leaving home, going to college, and/or obtaining a job. During this time when we are most significantly uprooted, we are also likely to make major decisions such as changing cities, becoming involved in a serious relationship, and exploring other lifestyles, political parties, and religions.

So as Generation Z reaches the late teenage years and ventures forth into the world, what kinds of forces are going to shape our perspective on the government and therefore our perspective on civil liberties? One obvious force is the understanding of how we form relationships. As we spend an increasing amount of our lives online, we see our lives in the virtual world as a natural extension of our real world. We expect the same rules to apply to digital life as to physical life. In other words, if law enforcement is not allowed to snoop into my house without probable cause, then why should they be allowed to snoop into my e-mail or texts?

In fact, surveys show that we in Gen Z are less tolerant of government surveillance than previous generations. Recent data from a Pew Research poll shows that there has been a 50 percent increase in the number of teens and those in their twenties who believe that anti-terror policies have gone too far in restricting civil liberties, up from 40 percent in 2010 to 60 percent in 2013.[8] In another Pew poll published in 2011, 72 percent of Millennials (those born between 1981 and 1993, who turned eighteen between 1999 and 2011), answered "No" to the question "To curb terrorism, will it be necessary for Americans to give up some civil liberties?"[9] All the other generations were evenly divided. Based on my experience, this trend continues from the Millennial generation to the following generation—my generation, Gen Z. Note that there is no exclusive polling data for Gen Z since most of us have not reached adulthood and thus have not yet been polled. However, extrapolating from the Millennial era is reasonable since there is a clear trend in one direction at this point.

The data on my generation's waning support for government surveillance programs is evident also in the aftermath of the 2013 Edward Snowden leaks of NSA material. Snowden, a former NSA contractor, committed what is considered the most significant leak to date in US history. A Pew/USA Today poll one year later showed that eighteen- to twenty-nine-year-old Americans were significantly more supportive of Snowden than those over the age of sixty-five and were the only age group in which a majority did not favor prosecution. Forty-seven percent of eighteen- to twenty-nine-year-olds thought he had served rather than harmed public interest.[10]

Outside of government surveillance, Gen Z also leans left on other issues related to civil liberties. Part of this has to do with my generation's tolerance of other views. Reexamining data from the Millennial generation, in a 2010 Pew survey, whites under the age of thirty concluded that they were more than fifty points more likely than whites over sixty-five to say they were comfortable with someone in their family marrying someone of another ethnicity or race.[11] And a 2011 poll by the Public Religion Research Institute found that almost 50 percent of evangelicals under the age of thirty back gay marriage.[12] Although here again there is no specific data yet from Gen Z, my experience with peers of my generation has been the same with regard to these views.

The shift toward the left of the political spectrum among Gen Z is predicted by the Pew Research, which recently noted that "in the last four national elections, generational differences have mattered more than they have in decades. According to the exit polls, younger Americans have voted substantially more Democratic than other age groups in each election since 2004, while older voters have cast more ballots for Republican candidates in each election since 2006."[9]

But the question one should ask is "Why does Gen Z lean toward the left?" In terms of social and environmental issues, the data is clear: the economy and educational opportunities are other issues that affect us most. And here again, it appears that Gen Z leans left. What about security threats in the post-9/11 world? Although this was a catastrophic event, it didn't necessarily affect all of us in Gen Z equally. Many of us were in our infancy during that event, and some of us were not even born. Yet economic and educational opportunities, or lack thereof, have continued to impact our families and us as we have grown up.

Given today's economy, there is less economic security yet limited government protection and more deregulation. The conclusion among many Gen Zers is that this leaves us growing up in an era of uncertainty, which in turn leads to the perspective that the government favors economic goals benefiting corporations over economic goals that favor the individual. This explains why, according to Peter Beinart, associate professor of journalism and political science at the City University of New York, Millennials favored expanding the Affordable Care Act by a margin of seventeen points, despite the fact that the majority of older Americans favored repealing it even after the Supreme Court upheld its constitutionality in 2012.[13]

Moreover, according to Beinart, additional polling data shows that younger generations are "far more likely than older Americans to say that business enjoys more control over their lives than government." Senator Elizabeth Warren from Massachusetts, a former law school professor specializing in bankruptcy, recently reinforced this view.

In a recent Senate banking committee hearing, she asked federal bank regulators why not a single bank was taken to trial in the aftermath of the Financial Crisis of 2008, which was considered to be the worst financial crisis since the Great Depression. She then admonished the regulators for a "too-big-to-fail has become a too-big-to-trial" mentality.[14]

Warren's popularity with young adults continued into the Democratic convention of 2014, where she stated that "we don't run this country for corporations; we run it for people." Given Gen Z's concern for the influence of corporations in government, this comment resonated with us. In addition, Warren addressed head-on another issue important for Gen Zers: the college loan debt. The very first bill she introduced as a senator was a proposal to charge college students the same interest rates for their loans that the Federal Reserve offers big banks.

As Gen Zers continue to grow into their late teens and early twenties—those years characterized by Karl Mannheim as the foundation of our adult views on life and society—political and business leaders on both sides of the spectrum will need to understand and accommodate for these perspectives. The reduction of student loan debt, the reduction of corporate influence on political decision making, the reduction of government surveillance in our lives, and tolerance of an individual's self-expression in society are the values that we will advocate as we reach adulthood.

Notes

1. Richard Spillet and Ryan Gorman, "Dutch Teen, 14, Is Arrested in Rotterdam after Tweeting 'Joke' Al Qaeda Bomb Threat to American Airlines," *Daily Mail*, April 14, 2014, http://www.dailymail.co.uk/news/article-2604387/Dutch-teen-ARRESTED-Rotterdam-tweeting-joke-bomb-threat-American-Airlines.html.

2. Caitlin Dewey, "Dozens of Teenagers Are Now Tweeting Bomb Jokes to American Airlines," *Style Blog, Washington Post*, April 14, 2014, http://www.washingtonpost.com/blogs/style-blog/wp/2014/04/14/dozens-of-teenagers-are-now-tweeting-bomb-jokes-to-american-airlines.

3. Jennifer E. Rothman, "Freedom of Speech and True Threats," *Harvard Journal of Law & Public Policy* 25, no. 1 (2001), http://www2.law.ucla.edu/volokh/rothman.htm.

4. Jon Ronson, "How One Stupid Tweet Blew Up Justine Sacco's Life," *New York Times Magazine*, February 12, 2015, http://www.nytimes.com/2015/02/15/magazine/how-one-stupid-tweet-ruined-justine-saccos-life.html.

5. Sam Biddle, "Justine Sacco Is Good at Her Job, and How I Came to Peace With Her," *Gawker*, December 20, 2014, http://gawker.com/justine-sacco-is-good-at-her-job-and-how-i-came-to-pea-1653022326.

6. "Theory of Generations: Karl Mannheim Flashcards," posted by "eepiukana," Quizlet LLC, published September 2014, http://quizlet.com/47236785/theory-of-generations-karl-mannheim-flash-cards.

7. *Encyclopedia.com*, s.v. "Karl Mannheim," accessed December 20, 2014, http://www.encyclopedia.com/topic/Karl_Mannheim.aspx.

8. Pew Research Center, *Few See Adequate Limits on NSA Surveillance Program*, July 26, 2013, http://www.people-press.org/files/legacy-pdf/7-26-2013%20NSA%20release.pdf.

9. Pew Research Center, *The Generation Gap and the 2012 Election,* November 3, 2011, http://www.people-press.org/files/legacy -pdf/11-3-11%20Generations%20Release.pdf.

10. Drew DeSilver, "Most Young Americans Say Snowden Has Served the Public Interest," *Fact Tank* (blog), Pew Research Center, January 22, 2014, http://www.pewresearch.org/fact-tank/2014/01/22 /most-young-americans-say-snowden-has-served-the-public-interest.

11. Pew Research Center, *The Decline of Marriage and Rise of New Families,* November 18, 2010, http://www.pewsocialtrends .org/files/2010/11/pew-social-trends-2010-families.pdf.

12. Public Religion Research Institute, "A Shifting Landscape: A Decade of Change in American Attitudes about Same-Sex Marriage and LGBT Issues," February 26, 2014, http://publicreligion.org /research/2014/02/2014-lgbt-survey.

13. Peter Beinart, "The Rise of the New New Left," *Daily Beast,* September 12, 2013, http://www.thedailybeast.com/articles /2013/09/12/the-rise-of-the-new-new-left.html.

14. Jake Zamansky, "Too Big to Fail Now Too Big to Stand Trial," *Forbes,* February 21, 2013, http://www.forbes.com/sites /jakezamansky/2013/02/21/too-big-to-fail-now-too-big-to -stand-trial.

Conclusion

I set out to write this book in order to learn a little bit about myself and my generation. After all, we have an inherent connection with others who have grown up in the same era, as we share common experiences and beliefs that are often rooted in pop culture and the current events of our time. We identify so strongly with our own generation that we are prone to developing misconceptions and stereotypes about other generations. I experienced this realization myself after many long discussions with my four grandparents, which helped dispose of my own prejudices about their generation. I have noted my gratitude for my grandparents' role in this in the acknowledgments section of this book.

Similarly, I hope that this book will dispel certain prejudices about Generation Z—a generation which represents one-quarter of the current North American population and whose influence on society is just beginning. By going beyond stereotypical labels such as "That kid is in his own world, tweeting away while listening to music with earbuds," the reader can hopefully better connect with a Gen Zer, whether that person is a neighbor, a relative, or a worker in the same business.

The influence of Gen Z lies in its ability to take advantage of technology, hyperconnectivity, and instant access to information, which could create a far deeper understanding of humanity than what could have been possible in any generation before. A global, deeper appreciation for humanity is the first step to achieving the goals I set out in my introduction: peace, love, happiness, and security. But while today's technology allows us to share our lives and experiences with anyone around the globe, this in itself will not lead to global relatedness.

As we addressed in part 1, there are certain concerns we must face when our lives become interconnected through technology. For example, we must grapple with technology's role in shaping the identities of individuals growing up in Gen Z. We must understand the unintended consequences of having too much personal information available for the world to access. And finally, we must have a discussion about the right to remove information about ourselves from online sources, including in this discussion the establishment of legal boundaries.

Once we establish who we are and how we can express ourselves in the online community, the sharing of our thoughts, hopes, and concerns will become more genuine. When we share truly and authentically, we expect others to relate to us in the same manner. Yet, as shown in part 2, our attitudes serve as filters that deeply impact our own thoughts and beliefs. Attitudes toward money, toward competition, toward learning, and toward political beliefs are just some of the bases by which we judge others and ourselves. Yet only by having a candid discussion about these attitudes—a topic we explored in part 3—can we alter them, or at least become aware of their influence on our own beliefs.

The better we understand the impact of our attitudes, the more sincerely we can relate to others. We will then be one step closer to using technology to truly understand humanity. It is at this point that sharing our lives and experiences across the globe will produce ideas and insights that generate ingenious solutions to the problems we face, such as climate change, racial and gender inequality, and civil liberties. Our identities, attitudes, and perspectives will shape the future—a future that is being increasingly impacted, as we speak, by Gen Z.

About
the Author

Vivek Pandit is an ordinary teen with extraordinary passions. Like many high schoolers, he walks in sneakers with headphones in his ears and sees endless possibilities. He is a devoted older brother who plays varsity football, does crew in the off-season, performs modern dance, and loves to make everyone laugh. In school, he enjoys psychology, math, and international studies. One day, he hopes to explore all seven continents—and maybe even another planet.